M000081961

WITHOUT A DOUBT

HOW TO KNOW FOR CERTAIN THAT YOU'RE GOOD WITH GOD

DEAN INSERRA

MOODY PUBLISHERS
CHICAGO

Some content in this book has been adapted from Dean Inserra, *The Unsaved Christian: Reaching Cultural Christianity with the Gospel* (Chicago: Moody Publishers, 2019).

Scripture quotations marked CSB have been taken from the Christian Standard Bible®, Copyright © 2017 by Holman Bible Publishers. Used by permission. Christian Standard Bible® and CSB® are federally registered trademarks of Holman Bible Publishers.

Names and details of some stories have been changed to protect the privacy of individuals.

Published in association with the literary agency of Wolgemuth & Associates.

Edited by Mackenzie Conway
Interior Design: Erik M. Peterson
Cover Design: Kaylee Lockenour

Library of Congress Control Number: 2020940742

All websites and phone numbers listed herein are accurate at the time of publication but may change in the future or cease to exist. The listing of website references and resources does not imply publisher endorsement of the site's entire contents. Groups and organizations are listed for informational purposes, and listing does not imply publisher endorsement of their activities.

ISBN: 978-0-8024-2360-3

Originally delivered by fleets of horse-drawn wagons, the affordable paperbacks from D. L. Moody's publishing house resourced the church and served everyday people. Now, after more than 125 years of publishing and ministry, Moody Publishers' mission remains the same—even if our delivery systems have changed a bit. For more information on other books (and resources) created from a biblical perspective, go to: www.moodypublishers.com or write to:

Moody Publishers
820 N. LaSalle Boulevard
Chicago, IL 60610

1 3 5 7 9 10 8 6 4 2

Printed in the United States of America

To my dad, who made me know without a doubt of my earthly father's and heavenly Father's love. May others know for certain of their heavenly Father's love.

CONTENTS

THE QUESTION THAT KEEPS YOU UP AT NIGHT

Assurance of salvation is a God-given confidence for every true believer in Christ of their present approval and future acceptance by their Father.

RAY GALEA

As a child, I was never a good sleeper. I remember lying in bed and jumping out to check if anyone was in the room. I'm not exactly sure who I was looking for, but the thought of some intruder being in my room kept me up at night. I would look in the closet, under my bed, and then jump back under the sheets, thinking about this mythical person, who never once showed up in my room. Eventually, I would fall asleep.

Clearly, I had some issues, and sadly there weren't melatonin "sleepy gummies" for kids available in the 1980s. Now as an adult, who puts my own children to bed, I have a different set of things I think about at night: decisions for my family and the church I pastor, how to navigate through a pandemic that has altered life for us all, presidential elections, and how my New England Patriots are going to play without Tom Brady leading the team. Unless you are like my wife who falls asleep the moment her head hits the pillow, many of us have thoughts that keep us up at night, or, at the least, pop into our minds before we fall asleep.

Thankfully, there is one major question that never keeps me up at night or causes me to lose even a millisecond of sleep, and that is the question of where I stand in my relationship with God. I have complete assurance of my salvation. I know that my standing with God is secure because of the work of Jesus Christ on my behalf. Those who have placed their faith in Jesus Christ and have repented of their sins should never lose a moment of sleep, wondering about the status of their salvation. Unfortunately, there are too many people who aren't able to experience the peace of God, which surpasses all understanding, which guards their hearts and minds (Phil. 4:7). There are others who have a false assurance, hedging their salvation on matters the Bible doesn't prescribe for saving faith. It is very common in evangelical circles to focus on one having the certainty of assurance regarding one's salvation. This is important but has caused a de-emphasis on the warning against possessing a false assurance, where one believes they are saved, when in fact they are not. Our very lives depend on not getting matters of eternal significance wrong. We must know without a doubt that we are in Christ and forgiven of our sins.

The majority of people I encounter are not atheists. Often, they are vague theists. They believe in a very generic god who resembles anyone from a divine Santa Claus figure to a distant force or moral compass. This generic god is not the God of Abraham, Isaac, and Jacob, who has revealed Himself to us through the Scriptures and ultimately through Jesus Christ.[1] Rather, the idea that there is a God, and that it matters somehow for the afterlife, lingers in minds and subtly haunts people. Attend any funeral and almost every single time you'll hear that the deceased is in a "better place" as friends and families share stories and memories of a loved one. We are not told what that better place is or how one qualifies to be there, but it is simply stated and assumed.

There are others who certainly believe in the God of the Scriptures, but live their lives wondering, "Am I good enough?" and "Have I done enough?" There are many people living with "Catholic guilt," and it is common for those who grew up in a conservative Christian home to have "rededicated" their lives at a church service, youth retreat, or revival service to make sure they are "okay" with God, just in case.

OUR VERY LIVES DEPEND ON NOT GETTING MATTERS OF ETERNAL SIGNIFICANCE WRONG.

In one of John's letters to the church, he claimed to have "written these things to you who believe in the name of the Son of God so that you may know that you have eternal life" (1 John 5:13). According to the Scriptures, it is clear that God does not want His children lying in bed at night wondering where they stand with their Creator. Sleepless nights concerning this are a problem of belief, not behavior.

There is a type of apprehension that is appropriate and needed. If one believes their relationship with God, and eternal life, changes by the day based on personal moral performance, sleeping smoothly doesn't make very much logical sense. There isn't a pillow soft enough to ease the uncertainty of whether one has been "good enough" for God that particular day or in one's whole life. God wants us to have real assurance, not a faulty one, but one where believers can walk in confidence knowing that their redemption has been accomplished and guaranteed by the seal of the Holy Spirit.

There are two matters that must equally be addressed regarding the assurance of salvation. The first is for believers who have been saved from the consequences of sin and made new creations (2 Cor. 5:17), yet still have an inclination to question their salvation. This often comes from their personal background where the grace of God was under-emphasized or an opposite extreme, which made salvation more of a rite of passage, such as being confirmed or merely praying a prayer as a child. While these individuals may know the Lord and possess eternal life, it is not surprising that a person from this type of background would wonder if real, genuine conversion was experienced, or if it was more of a ritualistic act participated in out of family tradition and expectation.

The other matter of concern is a false assurance, where a person may believe their standing with God is based on their morals, values, generic beliefs, and family heritage. This is the modern day example of Matthew 7:21–23, where the religious would plead their case before Christ based on their righteous practices rather than on the righteousness of Jesus Christ, who rebuked their false assurance by stating,

"Not everyone who says to me, "Lord, Lord," will enter the kingdom of heaven, but only the one who does the will of my Father in heaven. On that day many will say to me, "Lord, Lord, didn't we prophesy in your name, drive out demons in your name, and do many miracles in your name?" Then I will announce to them, "I never knew you. Depart from me, you lawbreakers!" (Matt. 7:21–23)

These self-identified lawkeepers, based on the keeping of religious standards, were lawbreakers, according to Jesus. Works of righteousness are works of iniquity if done to justify one's standing before God, apart from Christ.

Due to the COVID-19 pandemic, we've seen the world disrupted by a deadly virus. People are thinking more about their mortality and, as a result, where they will spend eternity. Perhaps you picked up this book because you now have your own questions. I remember visiting a church one Sunday morning as a college student. The pastor leaned over the pulpit mid-sermon and shouted, "Do you know, that you know, that you know, that you are saved?" Thankfully, if one is in Christ, they no longer have to critically think through or process that tongue twister question. It is nearly impossible to live the Christian life with joy if one is being kept up at night wondering where they stand with God. I am grateful that God gives us the ultimate melatonin, and that is actual assurance, knowing not only that we have salvation but that we are in Christ and part of God's family, securely, for eternity.

I wish for you that you would experience this joy of knowing what it means to have certainty regarding your personal salvation. I love the way pastor Charles Bridges speaking over 150 years ago put it, "that a full sense of acceptance with God grounded upon the Divine testimony is attainable—there can be no doubt."[2]

CHAPTER 1

THE CONFUSION: WHAT A CHRISTIAN IS NOT

According to the late theologian R. C. Sproul, "The main way that people acquire a false sense of assurance of their salvation is by having a false understanding of the way of salvation."[1] I am an example of someone who wasn't saved out of atheism, but rather from false assurance. Being falsely assured of one's salvation is grounded in ignorance, and this is precisely my story and linked primarily with my own church upbringing. I grew up going to church every Sunday, unless I was sick or out of town. Each night, our family would say a memorized prayer before eating dinner: "God is great, God is good, let us thank Him for our food." I owned a Bible, which was given to me after my confirmation at the neighborhood Methodist church, but I don't remember reading it. I knew about Noah and the ark, David and Goliath, and that Jesus helped a lot of people.

In middle school, a pretty girl invited me to a Fellowship of Christian Athletes (FCA) "huddle meeting." I played sports and believed in God, and did I mention she was pretty? So I went. FCA was a great time, and I went every week to the huddle meeting with other classmates. We would hear something the kids called a "testimony" from athletes who played football for the Florida State Seminoles, and I thought it was the coolest.

As the school year went on, it was time for the FCA fall retreat. I had never heard of one of those before. It was a one-day event in a camp-type setting held about an hour from where I lived. The thought of getting on a bus and spending the day with my friends and playing in sports competitions sounded like my type of thing, so I signed up as quickly as my parents agreed to let me go. After dodgeball, kickball, and some relay races, we had our assembly time. The speaker was a large man who had played professional football, and I remember thinking his muscles were bigger than Hulk Hogan's. He told really funny stories and then started talking about our need to trust in Jesus, that He died for our sins and rose from the grave.

Up until this FCA retreat, if anyone had asked me if I was a Christian, I would have said yes without hesitation. But if you had asked me why I claimed to be a Christian (nobody ever had), trusting in Jesus and that He died for me would not have been my answer. And as for sins? I didn't really have a concept of my sinfulness. I got in trouble every now and then, but I figured the real bad guys were people who were in jail and on the Russian tag team I would watch each Saturday in pro wrestling.

The speaker gave what I now know is called an "invitation" to respond to his presentation of the gospel. At the time, I had never been to an event where the speaker had asked anyone to "come forward" and trust in Jesus Christ. He counted to three and asked people who wanted to be saved from their sins by "giving their lives to Jesus Christ" to come forward. The preacher talked about the blood of Jesus and heaven and hell. He told the packed basketball gymnasium of middle school students that we needed to ask God to forgive us for sinning against Him, repent of our sins, and become followers of Jesus.

Dozens of students stood up and walked forward to meet with FCA staff members and give their lives to Jesus. I didn't move, because as far as I was concerned, I was a Christian. Sin, Jesus' blood, and my need for repentance were new things to my ears, but I was fairly certain I was okay. My reasoning was simple: I believed in God; I wasn't of any other religion (like Judaism or Islam); I went to church on Sundays; and I was in FCA. I had never thought about trusting in Jesus because nobody had ever told me I needed to do so, but I figured since I went to church already, I was fine and probably had already done all those things.

Then something happened that opened my eyes, truly freaked me out, and changed my life. The speaker said, "There is one more thing I want to share for some of you still in your seats." He then read the words of Jesus from Matthew 7:21–23.

Not everyone who says to me, "Lord, Lord," will enter the kingdom of heaven, but only the one who does the will of my Father in heaven. On that day many will say to me, "Lord, Lord, didn't we prophesy in your name, drive out demons in your name, and do many miracles in your name?" Then I will announce to them, "I never knew you. Depart from me, you lawbreakers!"

I don't remember his commentary exactly, but he shouted that there were people in the room who went to church, came from good families, said a prayer before meals, but had never trusted in Jesus Christ. "You are no more a Christian than someone who doesn't believe in God at all, and that will lead you straight to hell! God will not let sin go unpunished. You need forgiveness for your sins, and only Jesus can give you that forgiveness because He took on the punishment that you deserved, even though He had never sinned."

I know that's not always the best way to share the gospel, but it certainly got through to me. He gave a second invitation, and I believed he was speaking directly to me. I walked down to the front completely freaked out. I had thought hell was for really bad people who committed crimes like murder, not for someone like me. It is where evil dictators went, not middle-schoolers from nice families who went to church and had a picture in the Olan

Mills church directory to prove it. This muscular, enthusiastic preacher was talking about a Jesus with whom I was unfamiliar. "The gospel," in my mind, was a kind of music where people wore choir robes and clapped. I had no idea it was about Jesus dying on the cross for me or that His death even mattered. I walked forward, prayed to trust in Christ with a staff member named Walter, and I was angry. Don't get me wrong, I experienced joy over this great news about my sins being forgiven, but I was upset. How was it that I had been to church my entire life and nobody had ever told me this news?

THE SECURITY I NOW FELT WAS BASED ON TRUTH, NOT ON FAULTY ASSUMPTIONS THAT CLAIMED TO BE CHRISTIAN WITHOUT ANY DEPENDENCE ON THE SAVING WORK OF JESUS CHRIST ON MY BEHALF.

I needed someone to talk to me about assurance because I had no idea mine was false. In my eyes, I was headed to heaven when I died because that's where you go if you're not a bad person. I didn't lie awake at night thinking about my relationship with God because I didn't know I had any reason to worry about it. This is not because I was secure in Christ, but because I didn't even know what that meant or why it mattered. As I look back on my childhood, now as an adult, I realize my false assurance was due to my unclear beliefs. I assumed I was a Christian, but that was by culture, rather than by conviction. My assurance was not supported by what the Bible considers an actual saving faith.

If I had a moment like the people who Jesus spoke about in Matthew 7:21–23, I would have advocated for simply being a nice person, that I believed in God, wasn't part of another religion, and practiced some Christian traditions such as going to church on Sunday and saying a prayer with the family before dinner. I'm thankful I sat under preaching that day at the FCA retreat, preaching that wouldn't let my ignorant assumptions go unchecked. My false assurance moved to a belief in the gospel of Jesus Christ. The security I now felt was based on truth, not on faulty assumptions that claimed to be Christian without any dependence on the saving work of Jesus Christ on my behalf.

CHAPTER 2

BARRIERS TO BELIEF

I love to visit college campuses, especially their football stadiums. Growing up, I have the fondest memories of my dad driving our family an hour out of the way on summer road trips so we could visit major college football stadiums. We would hope a gate or door would be open so we could slip through it and run out on the field. I have carried that family tradition on with my owns kids. While it does cause my wife to roll her eyes from time to time, if we are anywhere near a college football stadium, you better believe we are taking the backroads to go see it, even if it means we get to our original destination later than planned. One such trip had us a short drive from Norman, Oklahoma, home of the national powerhouse

Oklahoma Sooners football team. I was excited to step into the stadium of many national championship teams and Heisman Trophy winners. When we got to the gate, I realized quickly that the usual sneak onto the field was not going to happen this time. There was a barrier to getting to see this college football treasure: a large, ironclad, locked gate. What a letdown!

Those closed gates reminded me of the two sets of gates and two roads that Jesus used to illustrate the paths to assurance: "Enter through the narrow gate. For the gate is wide and the road broad that leads to destruction, and there are many who go through it. How narrow is the gate and difficult the road that leads to life, and few find it" (Matt. 7:13–14). According to Jesus, salvation is for the few of those who have passed through the narrow gate and, as a result, have found life. The idea of the wide gate and the broad road leading to destruction fascinates me. Especially since Jesus claimed that many go through that gate and walk that road. What caught my attention is how closely this ties not only in sequence, but also in tangible example, to the strong words of rebuke and warning in verses 21–23. After Jesus talks about the narrow road, he doesn't go into an exhortation about atheism or pagan religions, but instead highlights false assurance as an example of the wide gate and broad, destructive road. It is important to clarify that atheists certainly have a false assurance that takes confidence in their own intellect and conclusions about God, but that is not the focus of Jesus at this moment in Matthew's gospel. Rather, Jesus locks in on those being led astray by false teachers or by being self-deceived by believing that their status with God is not a problem to be addressed.

Thankfully our fortunes changed the next time we found ourselves in Norman, Oklahoma. A friend made a phone call to someone in the athletic department who had a key, and they gladly let us in. It was an absolute thrill to run on the field where Heisman Trophy winner Billy Sims ran for touchdowns and the sound of the famous "Boomer Sooner" fight song echoed through the stadium Saturday afternoons in the fall. To pass through the gate, someone had to let us inside. While the Holy Spirit is the one who brings people into the narrow gate (John 6:63), Christians are called as God's ambassadors to agree to lead all those who will come to that gate and hand them the keys to get on the field.

Just like the closed and locked gate in Norman, there

CHRISTIANS ARE CALLED AS GOD'S AMBASSADORS TO AGREE TO LEAD ALL THOSE WHO WILL COME TO THAT GATE AND HAND THEM THE KEYS TO GET ON THE FIELD. are barriers on the road to assurance, and it is important to understand them for our own self-examination (2 Cor. 13:5) but also in ministering to others, desiring to see them pass through the narrow gate, onto the road that leads to life with Jesus Christ and full assurance of His grace. Christians should be running on the field of assurance rather than hoping they have the means to get through the gate. The following barriers keep the gate of assurance closed for many.

BELIEF

I am well aware that it appears strange at first to claim such a thing as belief can be a barrier to saving faith in Jesus Christ. Where false assurance can reign supreme is in the thought that since one isn't an atheist, agnostic, or a member of one of the world's other major religions, such as Judaism, Islam, or Buddhism, it must mean they are a Christian. James, in his New Testament letter, had something to say about this false assurance of mere belief when he matter-of-factly stated, "You believe that God is one. Good! Even the demons believe—and they shudder" (James 2:19). I can feel James saying, "Oh, you believe in God? Cool, want a cookie?" The demons actually would have had a right belief about much of the things of God. If anyone knew there is one God and His name is Yahweh, it is the devil and his minions. That reality is their worst nightmare; they hate that truth. At the barrier of belief, a right view of God is not what one will find. Sadly, the demons get it more right.

The god these people believe in is somewhere on the scale of being "the Big Man upstairs" or a grandfather-like figure, to a good luck charm or the Force from Star Wars. This god is generic and vague. One might ask, "Who are you to claim that someone's belief in god is not accurate?" While that is a fair question, the Scriptures are clear that God is not vague or generic. He has made Himself known to us by speaking, and the way He has revealed what He desires for us to know about Him is through the Bible. Assurance does not require everyone to become expert theologians; however, it does require us to believe in God as He has revealed Himself to be, not a god that we have invented or made up. It is important to ask oneself the questions, "Who is this God I claim to believe in, and from where did I gather this belief?" Believing in God does not make one a Christian. If that were the case, James says the devil would be doing just fine.

MORALS

Good people go to heaven. This might be the most common universal belief in America today. We aren't told what the standards are for being a good person or any details about heaven, but there is this imagined "better place" that apparently has an eighteen-hole golf course in the sky, where Uncle Bob plays every day. A major cause of false assurance is the confidence in one's own standing as a good person. What makes this an easy barrier to get trapped under on the road to the assurance of salvation is that this belief in oneself being a good person is usually correct by the world's standards of what it means to be moral, ethical, and an individual who possesses values. As long as you practice the moral version of keeping up with the Joneses, it is easy to believe that there is a grand golf course in the sky waiting for you to swing your golden driver at heaven's country club after you die and head to the better place.

Part of the issue is that the wrong comparison is being made. It doesn't make sense for a five-star steakhouse to compare itself to a fast food restaurant, or for that fast food restaurant to compare itself to an elite, fine dining restaurant. Those places aren't the standard for each other. When we compare ourselves to others, it is easy to believe that we are good people. When we compare ourselves to God, we fall short every single time. This wrong comparison issue goes back to the assurance barrier of belief in a generic or vague god. Sinning against "the Big Man upstairs" leaves one with no reason to worry when they sin. This god won't think it is a very big deal. This god functions as a Mother Nature figure or a divine Santa Claus figure. Worst case scenario, there will be coal in your Christmas stocking. God as a distant force leaves one without any fear. J. I. Packer wrote, "Unless we see our shortcomings in the light of the law and the holiness of God, we do not see them *as sin* at all."[1]

As a middle school student just starting my teenage years, I would have never considered myself a sinner. Did I occasionally do something wrong that would cause my parents to send me to my room all night? Yes, but what's the big deal? I served my punishment by missing out on the movie or whatever my friends were doing that weekend. I would have my privileges back on Monday morning. "Sinning" was something reserved for really bad people, like the ones I learned about in my mainline Protestant Sunday school. Goliath, Nebuchadnezzar, and Jonah (before the fish swallowed him)—those were the bad guys. I wasn't a sinner because I went to church, prayed before dinner, and did more good deeds than bad. I was also a member of the Inserra family, and we are good people, after all. It has been said that the most important thing is what comes to our mind when we think about God.

Based on my generic theism, and what came to my mind when I thought about God, I wasn't worshiping the God of the Bible. I was giving occasional nods to a superhero character who beat the bad guys in the Old Testament but was also kind of like Santa, who would answer my bedtime prayers if I stayed off the naughty list. Falling on the right side of the list usually meant not being that bad, like the bully at school or the kid who always got put in time-out during recess on the playground.

When other people are the standard of goodness, you can always find people a little worse than yourself. But when God is the standard, and I compare myself to Him, the only response can be, "God, have mercy on me, a sinner!" (Luke 18:13). That plea doesn't exist without recognizing the holiness of God. When we finally realize we are great sinners, we can finally understand that we have a great Savior. Paul claimed that if good people go to heaven based on their personal morals, then Jesus died for nothing (Gal. 2:21). I can't think of a more swing-and-miss belief when it comes to personal assurance of salvation than functionally believing that Jesus died for no purpose.

Of course, nobody claiming to be a Christian would ever admit they believed Jesus died for no reason, as that sounds so terrible, but the moment we believe our morals get us to heaven, we are holding up a large neon sign that declares the cross of Jesus Christ was worthless. Galatians 2:21 couldn't be clearer. To have assurance and an actual conversion to Christ, we must realize well-intentioned good deeds don't change the fact that we are sinners and need forgiveness. Comparing ourselves to others, rather than to God, is the theological version of "apples and oranges." A person who believes in God yet doesn't see the personal need of redemption is a person who should have the word "assurance" banned from their mind and vocabulary. There is nobody on the planet who should be less confident in their salvation.

HERITAGE

> **WHEN OTHER PEOPLE ARE THE STANDARD OF GOODNESS, YOU CAN ALWAYS FIND PEOPLE A LITTLE WORSE THAN YOURSELF. BUT WHEN GOD IS THE STANDARD, THE ONLY RESPONSE CAN BE, "GOD, HAVE MERCY ON ME, A SINNER!"**

A family heritage and tradition of faith can easily be confused with saving faith in Christ. It is often the case that the faith of the grandparents is respected but may be viewed as extreme or out of touch by the younger generation's of the family. So the younger generation rides the coattails of religious family members but pick and choose the things they like, adopting a more comfortable, casual form of faith in a generic god. I remember being told as a teen at youth camp that "God doesn't have grandchildren." As one who had a Christian grandmother, I needed to hear those words. My grandmother's faithfulness to Christ wouldn't get me into heaven. God has children, and those children are brought about through faith in Christ (John 1:12–13). A legacy of faith should be celebrated, but a faith that is inherited is no faith at all. There is a strong difference between the two. Assurance is not found in being physically born into Christianity; it is found by actually being born again (John 3:3).

The barrier to assurance of family heritage can often take comfort in rites of passage. This can consist of a first communion, confirmation, baptism by immersion as a young child, or even saying the "sinner's prayer." Looking back to these moments for peace of mind as adults can be a barrier to understanding the gospel if genuine conversion did not take place. These barriers provide false assurance. Jesus told Nicodemus, a man who certainly had the credentials of religious heritage, rites of passage, and accolades, "Unless someone is born again, he cannot see the kingdom of God" (John 3:3).

Generic theistic belief, good values, and religious heritage are pillars of false assurance. If one is going to know how they can be sure of salvation, it must first be clear concerning what does not bring salvation.

CHAPTER 3

ESSENTIALS OF SAVING FAITH

Essential and non-essential businesses became a new part of our vocabulary and understanding during the COVID-19 order to stay at home. Before the pandemic, those terms weren't ever considered in our minds as a classification. They were all just referred to as "businesses." Thankfully, our faith is not that way. When it comes to a saving faith in Jesus Christ, there are no new categories that have been established concerning what is essential for genuine conversion and assurance of salvation.

The essentials of saving faith begin with one's personal beliefs about Jesus Christ and how salvation is accomplished. God is not silent about what one must believe in order to be saved. Jesus said that entrance into the kingdom of God requires that one believes (Mark 1:15). It is critical to understand what in fact people must believe in order to be saved. Assurance begins with right belief. As Aaron Menikoff succinctly puts it, "Though this belief is more than intellectual adherence to sound doctrine, it is not less."[1] There are beliefs that Paul classified as being of "first importance," the essential business of the faith, made clearly toward the conclusion of his writing in 1 Corinthians: "For I passed on to you as most important what I also received: that Christ died for our sins according to the Scriptures, that he was buried, that he was raised on the third day according to the Scriptures" (1 Cor. 15:3–4).

In summary, the Scriptures are our source for what we must believe, and the gospel is the essential business. Jesus Christ died for our sins, He was buried, and He rose from the grave. If there was a NCAA basketball tournament style bracket for necessary Christian beliefs for saving faith, these would be the number one seeds. These beliefs cannot be a casual hat tip to the idea of Jesus, but actually must center on rightfully believing in the work of Christ as the Bible presents it, the only hope for sinners to be reconciled to God.

Peter preached his first recorded sermon at Pentecost, where he claimed that "everyone who calls on the name of the Lord will be saved" (Acts 2:21). Salvation begins with the acknowledgement of one's need to be saved from God's just punishment of sin, the consequence being death. This is how one must believe in the saving work of Jesus Christ. Rather than symbolic of the *cause du jour*, it was a substitutionary death in our place that caused God's wrath to be satisfied. Without the shedding of blood, there is no forgiveness (Heb. 9:22). In our place, condemned He stood.

This is a far cry from the Pharisee in the parable in Luke 18, who trusted in himself that he was righteous (v. 9). There is no assurance of salvation in the goodness of oneself or in the belief in Jesus as some sort of symbolic figure, if one is to "know with certainty" (Acts 2:36). We are not called for a generic faith in some abstract word called "faith," but faith in the Jesus Christ of the Bible, the Lamb of God who takes away the sin of the world (John 1:29). In Him we have redemption, the forgiveness of sins (Col. 1:14).

Paul also names the resurrection of Jesus as an essential business of Christianity, to the extent that he admits the entire Christian faith is a farce unless there is an empty tomb (1 Cor. 15:12–18). Our salvation depends on Jesus being alive. While His death was because of our sins, our justification was the reason for His resurrection (Rom. 4:25). Pastor Fred Zaspel says,

> Christ's resurrection *says* something. It is the announcement of his justification. He was vindicated of all the unjust verdicts against him, and he was vindicated with reference to his death, as he said, for sinners. He said he would give his life a ransom for many. He said he would give his life for the sheep. He said that by his death he would effect their forgiveness and bring them into fellowship with God. He said that in his death he would accomplish salvation for his people. And now in his resurrection God publicly announces that it is so.[2]

Easter Sunday is not a metaphor for new beginnings or a celebration of spring. It is the celebration of an essential Christian belief of first importance: Jesus Christ has been raised for our justification. Without the resurrection, there is no salvation, but thankfully He has certainly risen, "raised on the third day according to the Scriptures, and that he appeared to Cephas, then to the Twelve. Then he appeared to over five hundred brothers and sisters at one time; most of them are still alive, but some have fallen asleep" (1 Cor.15:4–6). It is

WE ARE NOT CALLED FOR A GENERIC FAITH, BUT FAITH IN THE JESUS CHRIST OF THE BIBLE, THE LAMB OF GOD WHO TAKES AWAY THE SIN OF THE WORLD (JOHN 1:29).

clear that Paul wanted the Christians to know this without a shadow of a doubt, as by his own admission, that there is no Christian faith or salvation without it. If there is no faith without the resurrection, it means there is everything for the believer's assurance with it, as Christ's resurrection guarantees ours. For just as in Adam all die, so also in Christ all will be made alive (1 Cor. 15:22). While there are certainly other doctrines of the Christian faith that matter greatly, the saving power of the gospel is found in what Christ has accomplished for sinners, and this is understood in His death and resurrection, the essential truths of first importance.

Jesus, beginning His public ministry, proclaimed that the kingdom of God was at hand. The response was not only to believe this in faith, but also to repent (Mark 1:15). The essential beliefs one holds to are evidenced by how one responds to the faith they claim to possess by the practice of repentance.

While believing in Jesus and His gospel are essential, He also included the call to repent, to turn from one's sin and follow Jesus and His teachings. At conversion, the Holy Spirit enters a sinner's heart, causing one to be born again and made new. This results in one believing and professing Jesus as Lord over oneself. Believing in Jesus means understanding that He is Lord and we are not. The acting out of this new reality is found in repentance, where the believer turns from allegiance to self and the world, to allegiance and worship of Jesus Christ.

Theologian and pastor Sam Storms defines repentance as involving "a heartfelt conviction of sin, a contrition over the offense to God, a turning away from the sinful way of life, and a turning towards a God-honoring way of life."[3] There is a new way of living, under the authority of Christ, that is a response to one's biblical convictions and faith. The act of repentance happens at one's conversion, but then continues as a daily practice for those who are followers of Jesus Christ. This is the evidence that one is saved. The Bible calls these good works of repentance "fruit." Jesus said that when it comes to Christians, you recognize them by their fruit (Matt. 7:20). We will discuss this fruit in greater length in chapter 5.

There are some well-known state nicknames that are known throughout America. My home state of Florida is known as the Sunshine State. Just to the north of us is Georgia, the Peach State. Texas is the Lone Star State. If James was writing his letter from America, he would be sitting behind a computer in Missouri, the "Show Me" State. You're a Christian? Okay, great; show me. "Someone will say, 'You have faith, and I have works.' Show me your faith without works, and I will show you faith by my works" (James 2:18). James isn't bragging or claiming varsity-level spirituality, he is declaring that faith without works is dead (James 2:26), it is useless (2:20), it can't even be considered faith. Sinclair Ferguson says that "high degrees of Christian assurance are simply not compatible with low levels of obedience."[4] If one fails to bear the fruit of obedience, the only conclusion that can be drawn is that he does not understand the gospel or have actual biblical faith. Comprehending the love of God is the means by which faithful Christian living takes place and is the grounds of repentance. It is God's kindness that is intended to lead to repentance (Rom. 2:4). To not repent of sin and bear fruit is tragically a failure to understand the kindness of God.

The essential business of the Christian are faith and repentance. They are linked together arm in arm in the message that Jesus preached. To have faith in Jesus is to know Him in His death and resurrection and to understand that "He died for all so that those who live should no longer live for themselves, but for the one who died for them and was raised" (2 Cor. 5:15). If these are what Paul, inspired by the Holy Spirit, declared to be the essential beliefs of the faith, it means that God is the one who declared them essential business. Without these beliefs of first importance, there is no salvation. Without repentance, there are no genuine beliefs.

CHAPTER 4

BLESSED ASSURANCE

It is evidently our Father's will that His children's complete acceptance should not be a matter of present uncertainty. He intends not only that we should reach heaven at last but that heaven should commence on earth in a state of conscious security and peace; not only that we should have eternal life, but that we should know we have it (1 John 5:13). As theologian Charles Bridges said, "The gospel—instead of forbidding this privilege—warrants, produces, and establishes it; for the conviction of the professor, the excitement of the slumbering, and the encouragement of the weak."[1]

To those who were truly born again, Jesus gave great words of assurance concerning their salvation: "This is the will of him who sent me: that I should lose none of those he has given me but should raise them up on the last day" (John 6:39). If you believe that God's will is perfect, and that Jesus isn't a failure in carrying out the Father's will, you know He is not exaggerating. Jesus promised that nobody is able to snatch His sheep out of the Father's hand (John 10:28). Those in Christ have been given salvation. It is a gift.

When a young couple breaks up after dating for a period of time, it is common practice for the former girlfriend to put everything the boyfriend ever gave her in a box, and in one last act of zing in protest, leave the box full of all her former gifts on his front porch. It is the ultimate act of "we are done, and this relationship is officially over." That might work for the dating world, but that's not how God handles the gift of salvation He's given to His children. Jonathan Edwards is believed to be the one who first said, "You contribute nothing to your salvation except the sin that made it necessary." This is very good news regarding assurance, since we didn't do anything to contribute to our salvation, we can't do anything to forfeit it. Martyn-Lloyd Jones describes the significance of being certain that God doesn't take back His gifts, claiming that professing Christians "should all be concerned about our assurance of salvation, because if we lack assurance, we lack joy, and if we lack joy our life is probably of poor quality."[2] Jesus said, "I am the gate. If anyone enters by me, he will be saved and will come in and go out and find pasture. A thief comes only to steal and kill and destroy. I have come so that they may have life and have it in abundance" (John 10:9–10). A primary goal of the enemy is to keep the children of God from enjoying the pastures of abundant life. One of the most cunning ways he attempts this is by getting Christians to question and doubt God's promises, especially the promise of eternal life. There is abundant life and green pastures for those who are resisting the devil by resting in the assurance of salvation. As pastor Ray Galea said, "Assurance of faith is important because it not only provides great comfort to believers but stimulates a life lived in joyful holiness, and unending praise to God."[3]

Assurance of salvation must be understood theologically. Our hope is not in sentimentality or just hoping it all works out. Our hope of assurance is a certain hope that is based on what our salvation accomplished in the moment of our conversion and also for eternity. For those who are in Christ, "God is for us" (Rom. 8:31). In his theological work *The Everlasting Righteousness,* Horatius Bonar wrote:

> If He is not on my side, and if I am not on His, then what can I do but fear? Terror in such a case must be as natural and inevitable as in a burning house or a sinking vessel.
>
> Or, *if I do not know* whether God is for me or not, I can have no rest. In a matter such as this, my soul seeks certainty, not uncertainty. I must *know* that God is for me, else I must remain in the sadness of unrest and terror. In so far as my actual safety is concerned, everything depends on God being for me; and in so far as my present peace is concerned, everything depends on my *knowing* that God is for me. Nothing can calm the tempest of my soul, save the knowledge that I am His, and that He is mine.[4]

During the years of 1618 and 1619, an international synod met in the Dutch city of Dordrecht. Approximately one hundred were present as some of the great formulations of the Reformation came and controversy over Arminianism was settled. The theological statements and convictions that came from the Synod of Dort are known as the Canons of Dort. Along with the Presbyterian Westminster Confession of Faith (1646), both historic statements of theological clarity speak to matters of assurance and essentially give the same three answers for the sources of assurance for those in Christ.[5] I call them the three musketeers of assurance.

1. "Assurance comes from faith in the promises of God."

I have never met one Christian who would ever suggest even for a moment that God lies. Just the thought of ever saying that God lies gives me the heebie-jeebies. That is precisely what happens when one doesn't believe in the assurance of salvation. It is believing that God has broken His promise, has lied. While we are told to "have mercy on those who waver" (Jude 22). There is a strong difference between struggles of doubt concerning faith and outright believing that when God told us He would be faithful to complete the work He started in us (Phil. 1:6), that He was either exaggerating, joking, or telling an outright lie. We must not only believe but also remember the promises of God for His children. Throughout the Old Testament, there is a common theme for God in speaking to His chosen people, "I am the LORD your God, who brought you out of the land of Egypt" (Ex. 20:2). Over and over again, to many generations of people— including ones who never experienced the exodus from Egypt—a variation of that reminder of God's faithfulness to His people is spoken to them by Yahweh. Every word of God proves true (Prov. 30:5).

By observing Passover, the Hebrew people would continue to remember the promises and works of God. For the church, we take the Lord's Supper in remembrance of the body and blood of Christ given to redeem His people. I remember hearing revivalist sermons from traveling evangelists who would tell those in the congregation that if they didn't know the exact time and moment they were saved, they might not be and need to get saved tonight. They would give an emotional filled invitation to come forward and be sure that they know, that they know, that they know, they are saved. What a different approach than what John took when he wrote to the church that "this is the testimony: God has given us eternal life, and this life is in his Son. The one who has the Son has life. The one who does not have the Son of God does not have life. I have written these things to you who believe in the name of the Son of God so that you may know that you have eternal life" (1 John 5:11–13). John says we can know not because of a moment, but because of Christ and that He has given us life. Our

OUR ASSURANCE IS NOT IN A PRAYER OR AN EXACT TIME AND DATE, BUT IN JESUS CHRIST.

assurance is not in a prayer or an exact time and date, but in Jesus Christ. Faith takes God at His word, being "fully convinced that what God had promised, he was also able to do" (Rom. 4:21, see also Heb. 11:1–2). As Bonar said, "For we are not saved by believing in our own salvation, nor by believing anything whatsoever about ourselves. We are saved by what we believe about the Son of God and His righteousness. The gospel believed saves; not the believing in our own faith."[6] Based on this truth, we can be assured that we are saved.

2. "Assurance comes from the testimony of the Holy Spirit, testifying that we are children of God."

For all those led by God's Spirit are God's sons. For you did not receive a spirit of slavery to fall back into fear. Instead, you received the Spirit of adoption, by whom we cry out, "*Abba*, Father!" The Spirit himself testifies together with our spirit that we are God's children, and if children, also heirs—heirs of God and coheirs with Christ—if indeed we suffer with him so that we may also be glorified with him. (Rom. 8:14–17)

In his modern-day Christian classic *Knowing God* J. I. Packer wrote,

If you want to judge how well a person understands Christianity, find out how much he makes of the thought of being God's child, and having God as his Father. If this is not the thought that prompts and controls his worship and prayers and his whole outlook on life, it means that he does not understand Christianity very well at all.[7]

Packer believes that our understanding of Christianity cannot be better than our grasp of adoption. Assurance lies in understanding that we are God's children. Plainly stated, He doesn't abandon His children. God has dealt with this great problem of alienation through adoption, taking a person from one family (or no family) and placing him or her in a new family—the family of God. As theologian John Murray said, "By adoption the redeemed become sons and daughters of the Lord God Almighty; they are introduced into and given the privileges of God's family."[8] Adoption emphasizes the new status of the Christian. "To all who did receive him, he gave them the right to be children of God, to those who believe in his name, who were born, not of natural descent, or of the will of the flesh, or of the will of man, but of God" (John 1:12–13). Understanding the doctrine of adoption should leave no doubt for the believer wondering about assurance, as it explains our new relationship to God and that we are now God's heirs with Christ. Adoption is one of the most helpful metaphors in our understanding of our salvation in Christ.[9]

We, who through the redemption accomplished by Christ, have received the Spirit of adoption are now children of God, and if children, then heirs of God and fellow heirs with Christ (see Rom. 8:15–17). Central to this adoption we have received in Christ is its irreversibility. We are not adopted for a term, but for eternity. We are no longer orphans but are now and forever, by the mercy of

THE ADOPTION WE HAVE RECEIVED IN CHRIST IS NOT REVERSIBLE OR CONDITIONAL—IT IS ETERNAL AND UNCONDITIONAL.

Christ, the children of God and heirs with Christ. The adoption we have received in Christ is not reversible or conditional—it is eternal and unconditional. Sometimes the most simple and plain answers are the best answers. I can't stop being a child of God because I am a child of God through adoption. This is not foster care, where I am taken care of by a family for a temporary season. My forever family is my heavenly one. As Galea states, "God wants His children to know they are His beloved (1Jn. 3:1–3), rather than stay in suspense as to whether He is for them or against them."[10]

3. "Assurance comes from 'a serious and holy pursuit of a clear conscience and of good works' (Canons of Dort 5.10)."

Theologian Louis Berkhof wrote,

There can be no doubt about the necessity of good works properly understood. They cannot be regarded as necessary to merit salvation, nor as a means to retain a hold on salvation, nor even as the only way along which to proceed to eternal glory, for children enter salvation without having done any good works. The Bible does not teach that no one can be saved apart from good works. At the same time good works necessarily follow from the union of believers with Christ.[11]

Good works flow from our union with Christ, as Jesus said, "The one who remains in me and I in him produces much fruit, because you can do nothing without me" (John 15:5). Berkhof adds that our works are "permanent validity" for the believer.[12] Packer writing on James' position on faith and works says, "When he says that one is justified by what one does, not by faith alone, he means by 'justified' 'proved genuine; vindicated from the suspicion of being a hypocrite and a fraud.'"[13] A genuine faith is proved by works.

An important question to answer for those who claim to be Christians or are wondering if their past conversion experience is genuine is whether they have shown past and present signs of repentance and are displaying fruit and good works but have seemingly left the faith. There are two different aspects when it comes to this scenario. There are those who apostate, meaning they have abandoned the Christian faith, and those who are rebelling but maintain the faith. Hebrews 6 has strong words for the apostate: "For it is impossible to renew to repentance those who were once enlightened, who tasted the heavenly gift, who shared in the Holy Spirit, who tasted God's good word and the powers of the coming age, and who have fallen away" (Heb. 6:4–6). Arthur Pink, commenting on this passage, states, "'falling away' which is here spoken of signifies a deliberate, complete and final repudiation of Christ—a sin for which there is no forgiveness."[14] Taking the passage as a whole, it needs to be remembered that all who had professed to receive the gospel were not born of God. The parable of the sower shows that. Intelligence might be informed, conscience searched, natural affections stirred, and yet there be "no root" in them. Pink adds that "all is not gold that glitters." John writing about those who ultimately leave the faith offered this insight to the readers of his letter, "They went out from us, but they did not belong to us; for if they had belonged to us, they would have remained with us. However, they went out so that it might be made clear that none of them belongs to us" (1 John 2:19).

Those who are in rebellion, who are Christians living in sin, are a different scenario and story. There have been many great works and commentary concerning the story of the prodigal son in Luke chapter 15.[15] Jesus tells this story to those who were complaining that He "welcomes sinners and eats with them" (Luke 15:2).

He also said, "A man had two sons. The younger of them said to his father, 'Father, give me the share of the estate I have coming to me.' So he distributed the assets to them. Not many days later, the younger son gathered together all he had and traveled to a distant country, where he squandered his estate in foolish living. After he had spent everything, a severe famine struck that country, and he had nothing. Then he went to work for one of the citizens of that country, who sent him into his fields to feed pigs. He longed to eat his fill from the pods that the pigs were eating, but no one would give him anything. When he came to his senses, he said, 'How many of my father's hired workers have more than enough food, and here I am dying of hunger! I'll get up, go to my father, and say to him, "Father, I have sinned against heaven and in your sight. I'm no longer worthy to be called your son. Make me like one of your hired workers."' So he got up and went to his father. But while the son was still a long way off, his father saw him and was filled with compassion. He ran, threw his arms around his neck, and kissed him. The son said to him, 'Father, I have sinned against heaven and in your sight. I'm no longer worthy to be called your son.'

"But the father told his servants, 'Quick! Bring out the best robe and put it on him; put a ring on his finger and sandals on his feet. Then bring the fattened calf and slaughter it, and let's celebrate with a feast, because this son of mine was dead and is alive again; he was lost and is found!' So they began to celebrate.

"Now his older son was in the field; as he came near the house, he heard music and dancing. So he summoned one of the servants, questioning what these things meant. 'Your brother is here,' he told him, 'and your father has slaughtered the fattened calf because he has him back safe and sound.'

"Then he became angry and didn't want to go in. So his father came out and pleaded with him. But he replied to his father, 'Look, I have been slaving many years for you, and I have never disobeyed your orders, yet you never gave me a goat so that I could celebrate with my friends. But when this son of yours came, who has devoured your assets with prostitutes, you slaughtered the fattened calf for him.'

"'Son,' he said to him, 'you are always with me, and everything I have is yours. But we had to celebrate and rejoice, because this brother of yours was dead and is alive again; he was lost and is found.'" (Luke 15:11–32)

The focus of the passage is Jesus speaking to the Pharisees, helping them to see that they are the entitled, older brother who does not have a proper understanding of grace, the Father's love and heart towards sinners, and, ultimately, the gospel. While New Testament scholars certainly point to the older brother's negative, graceless, and entitled response to the celebration of his rebellious brother's return home as the primary theme of Jesus' words in Luke's account, there is a part of the prodigal son story that stands out to me and has become my favorite aspect of the famous tale, and that is the rebellious son came home. The younger brother returned to his father. He realized there wasn't more to be gained by disobeying God than there was to be gained by obeying Him. This temptation dates back to the very first sin in the garden of Eden (Gen. 3:6). The prodigal son remembered who he was, repented, and returned home to his father, who received him with open arms. How do we know that those who have rebelled or wandered from the faith are secure in Christ? A great indication is that they repent of sin and return back to the God they claim to know. If you have found yourself in a place of rebellion against the Lord and have been running from Him, this promise also applies to you. Our Father invites His children to come home.

Paul took this matter seriously, to the point that he told the Corinthian church exactly how to handle matters when believers rebel against the Lord and are not quick to repent. "Hand that one over to Satan for the destruction of the flesh, so that his spirit may be saved in the day of the Lord" (1 Cor. 5:5). These are very strong words from Paul toward those in the church who were engaging in immortality "that is not even tolerated among the Gentiles" (1 Cor. 5:1). This concern for those in sin, and seemingly strong measures, were taken out of care for their souls and grounds for assurance. If they were actually part of Christ's church, eventually they will show that by no longer being in the flesh and actually showing they are saved. On the day of the Lord, God's judgement will not be upon them. "There is only one cure for a lack of fruit in our Christian lives. It is to go back to Christ and enjoy (yes, enjoy) our union with Him."[16]

CHAPTER 5

MARKS OF A TRANSFORMED LIFE

I have very fond memories of going to my grandparent's house as a child. My grandpa had two grapefruit trees in his backyard, and I remember climbing up the trees and picking the grapefruits when they were ripe and ready. My grandpa was very proud of his grapefruit trees and would box up the fruit and deliver them to his neighbors. I have driven by my grandparents' old house a few times since he and my grandmother passed away, and each time I thought about those grapefruit trees and wondered if they are still in the backyard. I have zero expertise whatsoever concerning fruit trees. My thumb is not in the same universe as one that would be considered green. I have never gardened nor planted a tree. You could say I am what they call "indoorsy."

Despite my complete lack of knowledge of hands-on experience regarding trees, I know for certain the trees in my grandparent's backyard were grapefruit trees. There is only one way I know this (and this will be the least deep truth you've ever read because it really is that simple by design). I know the trees in my grandparents' backyard were grapefruit trees because they had grapefruits on them. I would have never known they were grapefruit trees unless they had grapefruit hanging from the branches. Jesus instructed that it is when the Christian produces much fruit that they prove to be His disciples (John 15:8). The fruit is the evidence of one's confession of their essential beliefs about Jesus and His gospel. Another way the Bible explains fruit in the life of a Christian is by works or deeds done by those who claim to be in Christ. While the Scriptures make it clear that Christians have been saved by grace through faith, and this is not from ourselves; it is God's gift, not earned by works (Eph. 2:8–9), there is an expectation that the grace which has been received freely be evidenced in one's lifestyle.

James, writing to an audience who seemed to not be

producing fruit in their lives, asked, "What good is it, my brothers and sisters, if someone claims to have faith but does not have works?" He then asks the most important question about possessing faith in Christ even though works aren't present, "Can such faith save him?" (James 2:14). The answer to this sobering rhetorical question is no. This is not because one is saved by works, but because genuine Christian conversion into a new creation produces good works for the glory of God.

I believe it is important to give tangible examples of what a life lived by a saving faith actually looks like, rather than simply talk in theoretical terms. What are the fruits we should see in our lives that demonstrate a saving faith? In conversations with Christian friends, I have talked with many who had been having doubts about their spiritual lives. What does Christian faithfulness look like on a daily basis when everything you know has changed? Thankfully, we have a guide in the Scriptures that hasn't changed during the pandemic. Paul instructed the members of the Philippian church to work out their own salvation with fear and trembling (Phil. 2:12). This was not a call to do push-ups and Pilates in the fear of the Lord. It is a call to live a transformed life as God works His purposes through us. It is easy to say that, but what does it actually look like for the believer to live the transformed life?

A LIFE OF REPENTANCE

John Calvin once wrote that "repentance is not merely the start of the Christian life; it is the Christian life." A genuine Christian sees one's personal sin the way God sees it, as rebellion against Him. In His grace, God does not lead us to repentance with a judge's gavel, but through His kindness (Rom. 2:4). A life of repentance is not just a marker of someone who believes the gospel; it is also assurance that one actually understands the kindness and love of their heavenly Father. When we sin, there is great news for the child of God. In His compassion, God reminds us that "if we confess our sins, he is faithful and righteous to forgive us our sins and to cleanse us from all unrighteousness" (1 John 1:9).

GENUINE CHRISTIAN CONVERSION INTO A NEW CREATION PRODUCES GOOD WORKS FOR THE GLORY OF GOD.

ETERNALLY MINDED

T. D. Alexander explained the eternally minded fruit of Christian belief when he wrote, "Faith in the resurrected Son of God gives us confidence to trust that this life is but the prelude to something more wonderful."[1] Christians don't believe the lie that there is more to be gained by disobeying God than there is to be gained by obeying Him. We know that this world is not our home, so therefore our loyalties are not for this world, "for we do not have an enduring city here; instead, we seek the one to come" (Heb. 13:14).

SOUND DOCTRINE

Scott Swain says that "sound doctrine delivers us from the snare of false teaching."[2] There is a rotten kind of fruit that can be detected in an unregenerate person, and that is believing, holding to, and teaching a false gospel. Paul was so serious about the significance of sound doctrine that much of his New Testament letters consisted of instructing the church to make it an absolute priority. He instructed Titus that every elder must hold "to the faithful message as taught, so that he will be able both to encourage with sound teaching and to refute those who contradict it" (Titus 1:9). Knowing that a person believes what the Bible actually teaches certainly assures the believer in God's Word and spurs the Christian onto good deeds. "A man is justified by faith, but that he [also] ought to *know that he is justified*, and that this knowledge of justification is the great root of a holy life.[3]

SPIRITUAL DISCIPLINES

"Let's strive to know the LORD" (Hos. 6:3). Christians care about knowing Jesus more intimately, which comes through practicing spiritual disciplines designed for growth. Peter wrote to the church that "like newborn infants, desire the pure milk of the word, so that by it you may grow up into your salvation" (1 Peter 2:2). The first Christians in the book of Acts "devoted themselves to the apostles' teaching, to the fellowship, to the breaking of bread, and to prayer" (Acts 2:42). These were means God provided to help the believers grow in their faith and affection for God. As my faith and affection increase, my confidence in God should follow.

GENEROSITY

Jesus spoke with complete clarity on money, proclaiming that "where your treasure is, there your heart will be also" (Matt. 6:21). My heart is far from Christ if I am not living generously with regard to my financial resources. Paul wrote to the Corinthian church that God "loves a cheerful giver" (2 Cor. 9:7). A faithful Christian is one who learns to love what God loves, and the Scriptures are clear that generosity is near to the heart and character of God.

HEART FOR THOSE WHO DON'T KNOW CHRIST

Jesus told the scribes and religious rulers who did not understand why He spent so much time with sinners that a shepherd would leave ninety-nine sheep to go find one who was missing (Luke 15:1–4). A person coming to faith in Christ is the very thing that causes angels to rejoice in heaven (Luke 15:10). If we desire to be more like Jesus, we

AS MY FAITH AND AFFECTION INCREASE, MY CONFIDENCE IN GOD SHOULD FOLLOW.

must have a heart for those who need His salvation. A heart for the lost shows an awareness of our realization of our own stories of receiving the grace of Christ. Jesus said He came to seek and save the lost (Luke 19:10), and if we are in Christ, we will display the fruit of that same desire in our own lives.

LOVE FOR GOD AND HIS CHURCH

Jesus tells us that we show love for Him by obeying His commands (John 14:15). But we also see descriptions throughout Scripture of adoring God, praising Him, relishing in His grace. A maturing heart in Christ will grow more and more loving as it beholds our loving God. We also seek to love what God loves: His glory and His church. We see calls to continuously spur one another on to good works (Heb. 10:24), to only speak what benefits others (Eph. 4:29), to consider others more important than ourselves (Phil. 2:3), and to do good to all people, especially our Christian brothers and sisters (Gal. 6:10). The Psalms are full of adoring praises to God and the New Testament epistles are full of guidelines for interpersonal relations within the body of believers. Both elevate love and consideration above selfishness.

SHARING WITH OTHERS HOW THEY CAN KNOW THEY'RE SAVED

A side from human sin, if we could label one primary cause of both a lack of assurance and a faulty assurance, it's confusion over what the gospel is and what the gospel is not. It is trendy to claim that one needs to be known more for what they are "for" than what they are "against." While that suggestion certainly holds merit, oftentimes it takes understanding what something is not in order to grasp what something actually is. Communicating the gospel to those falsely assured or looking for actual assurance are both certainly in that category. What may sound simple and obvious to the mature gospel believer can be a point of confusion for those searching for clarity. It must be reiterated regularly that . . .

The gospel is not church attendance.
The gospel is not, "Be a good person."
The gospel is not theism.
The gospel is not heritage.
The gospel is not an ethnicity.
The gospel is not making Jesus your copilot or your lucky charm.

It must be made clear that personal efforts, perceived goodness, and religious activities are not the gospel of Jesus Christ so that those who are falsely assured Christians can be ready to understand what they've been missing, and those who know the Lord can be reminded of where true assurance lies and can be strengthened in their faith. The gospel is such good news that we must make sure we get it right. A false gospel doesn't bring assurance.

There are those who are falsely assured, but there are

brothers and sisters in Christ who need to understand the assurance they have in Christ. The question must be asked of those struggling with assurance, "Who can separate us from the love of Christ?" (Rom. 8:35). Paul goes on to give a fairly exhaustive list, to answer his rhetorical question, in a desire for the reader to understand the joy of knowing what God being for us means for our very lives.

Can affliction separate us from the love of God? No.
Distress? Not a chance.
Persecution? Nope.
Famine? Hardly.
Nakedness? Ask Adam and Eve; He gave them clothes.
Danger? Not even the worst kind.
Death? The last time I checked, the tomb of Jesus
Christ is still empty.

Nothing "will be able to separate us from the love of God that is in Christ Jesus our Lord" (Rom. 8:39). These are all a result of the opening verse of Romans 8, "Therefore, there is now no condemnation for those in Christ Jesus" (Rom. 8:1). This work of God to redeem His people was a process that started before time as we know it began as we know it. Romans 8:30 should provide comfort and confidence for the Christian regarding God's sovereignty and the outworking of His plan. Paul gives the process of how God has saved His people, saying "those he predestined, he also called; and those he called, he also justified; and those he justified, he also glorified" (Rom. 8:30).

God has predestined the believer for salvation.
God has called the believer to salvation.
God has justified the believer, making and declaring salvation.
God will one day glorify the believer, the eternal completion of salvation.

As Paul responded in the next verse, "What, then, are we to say about these things? If God is for us, who is against us?" (Rom. 8:31).

Those list of outcomes are simply questions and answers of assurance. Because nothing can separate the person that God is FOR from His love, we can be "sure of this, that he who started a good work in you will carry it on to completion until the day of Christ Jesus" (Phil. 1:6).

And just in case Paul didn't cover all the bases, he adds

"nor any other created thing" (Rom. 8:39). Talk about covering it all in one swoop!

The gospel is the word about Jesus Christ and what He did for us in order to restore us to a right relationship with God. As Tim Keller states, "Through the person and work of Jesus Christ, God fully accomplishes salvation for us, rescuing us from judgment for sin into fellowship with Him."[1] God has done what we couldn't possibly have done for ourselves: full salvation through the life and sacrificial death of His perfect Son, an ever-sufficient substitutionary atonement for our sins. If the children of God could lose their status with their Father, we would have already done so, over and over again, but thankfully, according to God's Word, "the hope of eternal life that God, who cannot lie, promised before time began" (Titus 1:2), nothing can separate the genuine believer from that promise or God's love. This love is available to you, today. Trust in Christ, repent of your sins, and never have to wonder where you stand with God again.

NOTES

Introduction: The Question That Keeps You Up at Night

Epigraph: Ray Galea, "Assurance," The Gospel Coalition, https://www.thegospelcoalition.org/essay/assurance/.

1. Hebrews 1:1–3.
2. Charles Bridges, *An Exposition of Psalm 119: An Illustrative of the Character and Exercises of Christian Experience* (London: R. B. Seeley & W. Burnside, 1835), 462.

Chapter 1: The Confusion: What a Christian Is Not

1. R. C. Sproul, *In Truths We Confess: A Systematic Exposition of the Westminster Confession of Faith* (Sanford, FL: Reformation Trust Publishing, 2019), 393.

Chapter 2: Barriers to Belief

1. J. I. Packer, *Evangelism and the Sovereignty of God* (Downers Grove, IL: InterVarsity, 2008), 68.

Chapter 3: Essentials of Saving Faith

1. Aaron Menikoff, "How Much Theology Do I Have to Know to Be a Christian?," The Gospel Coalition, August 11, 2018, https://www.thegospelcoalition.org/article/tgc-asks-much-theology-know-christian/.
2. Fred Zaspel, "Jesus' Resurrection, Our Justification," The Gospel Coalition, https://www.thegospelcoalition.org/essay/jesus-resurrection-our-justification/.

3. Sam Storms, "The Christian and Repentance," The Gospel Coalition, https://www.thegospelcoalition.org/essay/the-christian-and-repentance/.
4. Sinclair Ferguson, *The Whole Christ: Legalism, Antinomianism, and Gospel Assurance—Why the Marrow Controversy Still Matters* (Wheaton, IL: Crossway, 2016), 201.

Chapter 4: Blessed Assurance

1. Charles Bridges, *An Exposition of Psalm CXIX: As Illustrative of the Character and Exercises of Christian Experience* (London: Seeley & Burnside, 1850), 470.
2. D. Martyn-Lloyd Jones, *Romans: An Exposition of Chapter 8:5–17, The Sons of God* (Edinburgh: Banner of Truth, 1974).
3. Ray Galea, "Assurance," The Gospel Coalition, https://www.thegospelcoalition.org/essay/assurance/.
4. Horatius Bonar, *The Everlasting Righteousness: Or, How Shall Man Be Just with God?* (London: J. Nisbet & Co, 1873), 163–64.
5. Galea, "Assurance."
6. Bonar, *The Everlasting Righteousness*, 173–74.
7. J. I. Packer, *Knowing God* (Downers Grove, IL: InterVarsity Press, 2011), 201.
8. John Murray, *Redemption Accomplished and Applied* (Grand Rapids, MI: Eerdmans 1955), 132.
9. Albert Mohler, "When Adoption Fails, the Gospel Is Denied," AlbertMohler.com, April 20, 2010, https://albertmohler.com/2010/04/16/when-adoption-fails-the-gospel-is-denied.
10. Galea, "Assurance."
11. Louis Berkhof, *Systematic Theology* (Grand Rapids, MI: Eerdmans, 1996), 543.
12. Ibid., 543.

13. J. I. Packer, *Concise Theology: A Guide to Historic Christian Beliefs* (Carol Stream, IL: Tyndale, 2001), 161.
14. A. W. Pink, *An Exposition of Hebrews* (New York: Start Publishing, 2013).
15. See the writings of theologians such as Edmund Clowney and Tim Keller.
16. Derek Thomas, "Evidence of Assurance," *Tabletalk*, July, 2016, https://tabletalkmagazine.com/article/2016/07/evidences-assurance/.

Chapter 5: Marks of a Transformed Life

1. T. D. Alexander, "Be Heavenly Minded So That You're of Earthly Good," The Gospel Coalition, April 18, 2018, https://www.thegospelcoalition.org/article/heavenly-minded-youre-earthly-good/.
2. Scott Swain, "What is Doctrine?," Ligonier Ministries, May 1, 2015, https://www.ligonier.org/learn/articles/what-doctrine/.
3. Horatius Bonar, *The Everlasting Righteousness: Or, How Shall Man Be Just with God?* (London: J. Nisbet & Co, 1873), 149.

Conclusion: Sharing with Others How They Can Know They're Saved

1. Tim Keller, "The Gospel in All Its Forms," Acts 29, May 23, 2008, https://www.acts29.com/tim-keller-explains-the-gospel/.

WHAT TO DO WHEN THEY SAY THEY'RE CHRISTIAN BUT DON'T KNOW JESUS

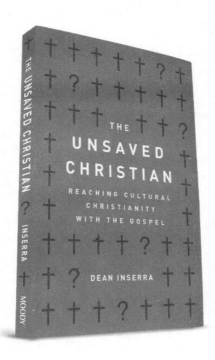

"What a___
in this room!"

Zarah whirled around at the sound of Stein's angry voice. "It's not what you think," she spluttered. "I wasn't trying to steal!"

Stein grabbed her wrists. "I saw you!" he thundered.

"You saw me looking for a photograph of my aunt," Zarah protested, too incensed to hide the truth. "Now let me go!"

"With pleasure," Stein retorted as he reached for a drawer, removed a framed photograph and thrust it into Zarah's hands.

Love for her dead mother welled up as Zarah studied the family resemblance.

"Tears?" Stein grunted skeptically.

"My aunt," Zarah replied, fighting for control. "She reminds me of my mother."

Unexpectedly Stein murmured, "Beauty, Zarah, appears to run in your family."

The man was too much! Zarah fumed. A compliment from his lips when all she'd heard up to now was the exact opposite!

Jessica Steele first tried her hand at writing romance novels at her husband's encouragement two years after they were married. She fondly remembers the day her first novel was accepted for publication. "Peter mopped me up, and neither of us cooked that night," she recalls. "We went out to dinner." She and her husband live in a hundred-year-old cottage in Worcestershire, and they've traveled to many fascinating places—such as China, Japan, Mexico and Denmark—that make wonderful settings for her books.

Books by Jessica Steele

HARLEQUIN ROMANCE

2494—BUT KNOW NOT WHY
2502—DISHONEST WOMAN
2555—DISTRUST HER SHADOW
2580—TETHERED LIBERTY
2607—TOMORROW—COME SOON
2687—NO HONOURABLE COMPROMISE
2789—MISLEADING ENCOUNTER
2800—SO NEAR, SO FAR
2850—BEYOND HER CONTROL

HARLEQUIN PRESENTS

717—RUTHLESS IN ALL
725—GALLANT ANTAGONIST
749—BOND OF VENGEANCE
766—NO HOLDS BARRED
767—FACADE
836—A PROMISE TO DISHONOUR

Relative Strangers
Jessica Steele

Harlequin Books

TORONTO • NEW YORK • LONDON
AMSTERDAM • PARIS • SYDNEY • HAMBURG
STOCKHOLM • ATHENS • TOKYO • MILAN

Original hardcover edition published in 1987
by Mills & Boon Limited

ISBN 0-373-02861-X

Harlequin Romance first edition September 1987

CHAPTER ONE

ZARAH had met the middle-aged Pearsons at her stop-over hotel the night before. They proved to be a delightful couple. Their friendliness, when the butterflies had started to attack, was just what she needed. Fresh off the Newcastle to Bergen ferry, her quest underway with no turning back now, she felt it was a help to have someone to talk to.

Not that she had breathed a word of her true reason for visiting Norway. So far as they knew she was on her way, after her widowed mother's death a month ago, to spend a holiday with an aunt who lived in Dalvik.

'Dalvik,' Mr Pearson had repeated, 'that's on the Tunnhovdfjord, isn't it?'

Zarah had learned that he and his wife knew Norway well. Indeed, so enchanted were they by the country that they missed a holiday every other year in order to save for a bi-annual motoring tour around the country they loved so well.

She saw Mr and Mrs Pearson again the next morning, Friday, when at breakfast in the crowded hotel restaurant, Mrs Pearson called her over.

'I've saved you a seat,' she greeted her. 'We were hoping to see you before you left.' It transpired that she must have been the subject of some small discussion between the parental couple, for as Zarah sat down with them, Mrs Pearson went on, 'We're making for Geilo today, and Norman says Geilo isn't all that far from Dalvik. We can give you a lift to your aunt's home if you like.'

Zarah had intended to take the train to Geilo, but since Dalvik did not appear on her train time-table, she had worried how she was going to make the twenty or so miles from there. English seemed to be spoken by everyone she had so far met, but that was not to say how she would fare in a more rural area.

'Are you sure?' she asked.

'Positive.' Mr Pearson's smile matched his wife's. 'You said last night that you weren't being met anywhere.'

'My visit to my aunt is a surprise visit.' Zarah returned his smile, and hoped her smile hid her anxiety that her visit might be more of a shock to her aunt than a surprise.

By six o'clock that day, although Zarah had not changed her opinion that the Pearsons were a charming couple, she had begun to wish she had stuck to her original plan.

She owned she was nervous about introducing herself to her aunt. But had she taken the train to Geilo, somehow or other she would be in Dalvik by now, and that first meeting with her Aunt Anne would be over.

As it was, the time was going on, and they had not reached Geilo yet. First Mr Pearson had insisted they must take in the atmosphere of the fish market. Then a ride to the top of the city on the funicular was a must. Late leaving Bergen, Zarah had known nothing of the twisting and winding roads in Norway that ensured no one could go anywhere at speed. To make their progress slower than ever, Mr Pearson dawdled in his determination that none of them should miss any of the superb scenery which lay around every bend.

Anxiety gnawed away at Zarah and left her without appetite when they stopped, and lingered, first for lunch, and then for a tea break. When at eight o'clock that night they reached Geilo and Mr Pearson said jovially he would check himself and his wife into their hotel before continuing on to Dalvik, so Zarah's anxiety peaked.

'I'm sure I'll be able to get a taxi to take me the rest of the way,' she said quickly, but added lamely, in view of their kindness, 'you might miss dinner if . . .'

'We're known here,' chorused both Pearsons happily as they arrived outside a hotel. 'They'll find us something to eat, no matter how late it is.'

They had been travelling some miles on the last leg of Zarah's journey, when conversation became spasmodic, and then petered out altogether. It was then that Zarah had space for her head to be filled with questions. It was then that she was filled with apprehension at what lay in front of her. But she could not turn back.

Like it or not, she had been born with an enquiring mind. Once her enquiring mind had taken her along the path it had, she had known no peace. Just as she knew there would be no peace until the questions triggered off by that piece of paper had been answered.

How she was going to feel when she had the answer to the one question that dominated all others, she did not know. What she did know was that something inside her refused to let go until that question *had* been asked.

Until as short a time as two weeks ago, she had not thought to question, but had always accepted as fact everything she had been told.

She was Zarah Thornton, only child of Margaret and Felix Thornton. Her mother had been thirty-six when smooth-talking Felix Thornton had waltzed into her life, married her, then quickstepped smartly out again when, uncaring for responsibility, he had learned that his wife was pregnant. Margaret had heard some months later that he had been killed in a light aircraft flying accident. Within hours of receiving that news, she had given premature birth to a sickly daughter who, because of some inoperable problem, it was thought would never walk.

Zarah had no memory of being in hospital until she was two years old. Though the almost invisible scar she carried was proof that her problem had not been so inoperable as had been first thought. Indeed, so successful had her surgery been that, able to walk tall and straight, she showed no sign now that there had ever been anything the matter with her.

Zarah switched to concentrate her mind on more facts as she knew them. Her mother had one sister, Anne. Anne had been a late child, and had been born seventeen years after her sister Margaret. Either the parents of the two sisters had run out of ideas by then, or perhaps they had been just following some whim, but where they had called their first child Margaret Anne, they had named their second child Anne Margaret.

In any event, with Margaret tied up with daily visits to see her premature baby in hospital, it had been Anne who had gone to register the baby's birth. It had been a family joke that Anne, in telling the registrar that she was Anne Margaret Gentry come to register the birth of a daughter to Margaret Anne Thornton, must have confused the poor man thoroughly. Because the name which appeared on Zarah's birth certificate in the section 'Mother' was that of Anne Margaret.

Zarah had grown up in the belief that the two sisters, probably because of the gap in their ages, were not very close. True, Anne had gone to live with Margaret in her Norfolk home when, forced to leave her baby in hospital for treatment, she had been discharged from the maternity ward.

A year later, Anne had met a Norwegian divorcee. Haldor Kildedalen was some years her senior, and in need of a housekeeper. She had gone to Norway with him, and six months later, she had married him. She never returned to England.

Not long after Anne's marriage, Margaret had found a French surgeon who was confident he could successfully operate on Zarah. The operation was a one-hundred-per-cent success, and a month or so later Zarah was allowed to go home. It was not to the Norfolk home that her mother had taken her, however. For in the meantime, an elderly aunt of the two sisters had died and had left them her cottage jointly. Zarah's first and only home was in Shrewsbury.

Zarah was aware that occasional correspondence passed between England and Norway. All letters were treated as private in their home, though. And although her mother would mention something or other that Anne had written, she had never actually given her any of Anne's letters to read.

Gifts were exchanged at Christmas and birthdays, with Zarah included and participating in such events. She had been about ten years old, she recalled, when at Christmas she had asked, 'Shall I write to thank Aunt Anne for her gift?'

Maybe it was because her mother never hesitated when it came to good manners that even now Zarah could recall that long moment of hesitation before her mother had replied, 'Yes, of course, dear. Your aunt would like that'. Her mother, an arthritis sufferer, had than struggled out of her chair and left the room to leave her to compose her own letter to her aunt in Norway.

By the time Zarah was fifteen, her mother's arthritis was so bad that some days she could not walk at all. When Zarah left school, Margaret Thornton was more or less confined to a wheelchair. But, brave soul that she had been, she was insistent that she would be perfectly all

right left alone all day while Zarah pursued some career
or other.

'No way,' Zarah replied, having inherited an ability to
dig her toes in too. 'What would I want with a career?'

'You've a fine brain, Zarah,' Margaret still insisted.
'You should be using it. You should be out meeting and
mixing with people of your own age. You should . . .'

Zarah had answered all her arguments. But when her
mother still did not look ready to accept that she wanted
to stay home and look after her, another thought
suddenly struck her.

'It's not money, is it?' she asked quickly, having no
recollection of money ever being tight in their home.
'You're still receiving your quarterly payment from
Grandfather Gentry's trust fund? I mean, I'll willingly
get a job if . . .'

'Our finances have never been more sound,' Margaret
Thornton stated promptly. 'We've got absolutely nothing
to worry about on that score. It's just that I—I don't want
to be a burden to you.'

'Oh, *Mum*!' Zarah had been aghast. And, because she
could not help it, she had gone to put her arms around
her, and had cuddled and coaxed, until finally Margaret
Thornton had given in.

They had lived happily over the next years, with
Margaret trying to retain much of her independence but,
because of her disability, having to rely on Zarah more
and more.

Zarah had been twenty-two when, a month ago, she
had hurried home from doing the weekly shopping to
find her mother had suffered an accident. Horrified,
Zarah had first seen the upturned wheelchair outside the
back door, and had raced over to it. Beneath the
wheelchair lay her mother, unconscious. She had never
regained consciousness, and died a few hours later in

hospital. It had appeared that, still striving to hang on to
her independence, she had apparently decided to take
something out to the dustbin. But in negotiating her
wheelchair down the ramp, then leaning forward to the
bin, she had tipped out of her chair and had hit her head
on the concrete slab.

Numbed as she was by her death, it was not until the
next day that Zarah realised she should inform other
people that Margaret had not survived the accident. But
then she realised that the neighbours already knew, and
there appeared to be only one other person she should
tell. Aunt Anne.

Dreadfully upset as she was, Zarah felt a decided
aversion to talking about what had happened. That,
coupled with the belief that her mother and her aunt were
not all that close, made Zarah opt to write rather than to
telephone Norway.

Two weeks later she took her courage in both hands
and went to attend to her mother's personal possessions.
She would have given anything not to have to be the one
to pack and dipose of her mother's belongings, yet at the
same time, it was unthinkable that she let anyone else do
it.

It was a harrowing task, a task which had Zarah
fighting against tears many times. But at last the
wardrobes were empty, and she next tackled a low chest
of drawers. That done, afraid if she left the room it might
be weeks before she found more courage to come back
and finish, she went to a taller chest of drawers that had
stood in the same spot ever since she could remember.
Working from the bottom up, she cleared each drawer in
turn, until she came to the top drawer. She had to
overcome a moment of weakness when she considered
how, with her mother unable to stand without assistance

latterly, it must have been some time since that particular drawer had been opened.

Zarah surfaced from her weak moment to pull open the drawer, to see that it held an assortment of papers. Weakness assaulted her again when the assortment turned our to be items which her mother had kept from sentiment. Items such as her first paintings from school, a school production Christmas card, signed 'To Mummy, love, Zarah!' If Zarah had not realised before, she knew then how very much her mother had loved her.

Suddenly a kind of peace came over her, and she was able, without tears, to work on until the drawer was empty. She was just about to close it, though, when she saw the shadow of another piece of paper that had slipped beneath the tissue lining.

She extracted it, to see that it was a copy of her mother's marriage certificate. Her glance slid past the date, and a wisp of a smile appeared on her mouth as she was reminded of the family joke about her birth certificate. The two sisters' names had been confused again, by another registrar, she saw. According to to this registrar, Felix Thornton had married Anne Margaret Gentry, and not her mother. This registrar was double faulted, she observed, for although it must have been Aunt Anne who had witnessed the ceremony, he had not written A.M. Gentry, but M.A. Gentry.

Zarah tidied up, and was on her way from the room when, for no tangible reason, she felt the most urgent pull to go back and take another look at the marriage certificate.

This time she read it more thoroughly, Then, for some moments, her brain seemed to refuse to function altogether. Stunned, she realised what had prompted her to take a closer look at the marriage certificate. She had grown up not questioning her mother's explanation about the mistake on her birth certificate. One mistake on a legal document had always than seemed quite feasible, but—two mistakes?

Not crediting the intelligence that was staring her in the face, all at once Zarah was starting to question, and question and question. Apart from the age of the bride being stated as nineteen, and not thirty-six, there was much else wrong!

Before she had given her birth, her mother had worked in an accountant's office. Arthritis had troubled her even then, so there was no way in which she could have taken a job which involved standing on her feet all day. Yet, according to this marriage certificate, under the heading 'Rank or Profession' the bride's job title was not 'Audit clerk', but—'Sales assistant'!

A memory floated into Zarah's head of a time when she had sat puzzling out some complicated maths homework, and had asked her mother's help. In no time her mother had worked out the problem and had explained it to her in simple terms.

'You're a genius,' Zarah had thanked her.

Her mother had grinned. 'I didn't spend all my working career in an accountant's office for nothing,' she had said.

The memory faded, but it had brought Zarah concrete evidence that her mother had never been the sales assistant stated on the marriage certificate.

A minute later, still stunned, Zarah was having her love and loyalty to her mother pulled at in all directions. For, if she was to believe the evidence of her eyes, then it was not her mother who had married Felix Thornton, but *Aunt Anne*!

Zarah attempted to scoff at the notion. She was emotionally out of gear from losing her mother, and was getting things out of perspective, she told herself. But try as she might to recall any conversation in which her mother had mentioned her wedding day, Zarah could not. Common sense told her that with the way the marriage had turned out it was no wonder that the subject was taboo. But as she pressed on, suddenly, and with fresh shock, Zarah found she was asking—and hating herself for the thought—if it had indeed been Anne who had married Felix Thornton, and if Felix had cheated Anne—with her sister! Was that the reason Felix had vanished the moment Margaret had told him she was pregnant? Was that the reason why Anne had left for Norway, never to return? Had Anne when she had found out . . .

Abruptly Zarah checked her thoughts. Her memory of her mother was precious, and she just could not believe that of her. She was aware from newspaper stories that people were capable of almost anything in the passion of the moment. But, remembering her mother, the standards she had held and had set, Zarah was certain her mother had been incapable of cheating anyone. Besides which, Anne had not left for Norway until Margaret's child was a year old.

Which had to mean that Margaret had not deceived her. Was it likely anyway that, had she been deceived, Anne would ever talk to her again, much less move in with her at that Norfolk home? Even far less would Anne go to the registrar's office on her behalf, to register the birth of a daughter from that deception. It would be much more likely for Anne to . . .

In mid-stream, Zarah's thinking side-tracked. All at once something of such staggering proportions struck her that she gasped aloud. She shook her head as if to clear it, but the new thought was still there and would not go away. Suddenly then, the question of whether it had been her mother or her Aunt Anne who had exchanged marriage vows with Felix Thornton had paled under this new and far more mind-boggling thought.

While there was no doubt who her father was, her birth certificate named not Margaret Anne as her mother—but Anne Margaret! Reeling, Zarah realised that if she were to believe the paper evidence, the legal paper evidence, it was not Margaret who had given her birth—but Anne!

A week went by with the question of whether she was the product of a marriage between Anne and Felix following her wherever she went. Even when she went to bed at night there was no rest from it. All her life she had known Margaret as her mother and still thought of her as her mother, yet had it been Anne who had married Felix and had given birth to her?

Another few days went by, with more questions presenting themselves. Everyone had called her mother Mrs Thornton. Did her mother have a legal right to call herself by that name? Or was it a name her mother had adopted when they had moved from Norfolk to Shrewsbury?

When, almost four weeks after her mother's death, still no reply had come to the letter she had written to her aunt informing of her sister's death, Zarah knew there was not going to be any reply. Plainly Aunt Anne, if aunt she be, had no wish to correspond with her niece in England. Just as plainly, Zarah knew that the answers to the questions that badgered away at her from morning till night were never going to be answered—not unless she asked the only other person who could tell her.

It was later the following afternoon when Zarah, who had not known a moment's peace in the two weeks since she had discovered that marriage certificate, knew she would have to take some sort of action, or go mad.

Her first impulse was to send another letter to Norway,

but she rejected the idea on the grounds that her aunt might well not reply to that letter either. Her next impulse was to telephone. That impulse was rejected too when she considered that Haldor Kildedalen might be the one to answer the phone. What if Anne had not told her husband anything of her past? What if, all these years, she had kept secret from him the fact that she had borne a child? To Zarah's way of thinking, the whole issue appeared shrouded in so much secrecy that anything was possible. The last thing she wanted was to stir up trouble for her aunt. Yet, when nightfall came, there was still something in Zarah which refused to let go until she knew the truth.

By morning, she knew what she was going to do. Grandfather Gentry's trust fund would cease now that her mother was dead, so Zarah knew she would soon have to get a job. Before she did that, however, there was something of a more pressing nature to be done. She had little in the way of savings, but by her calculations, it should be enough to get her to Norway and back.

'Dalvik.' Mr Pearson half turning in the driver's seat to tell her that they had arrived in the village of her destination brought Zarah rapidly to the present. Her stomach lurched, and her mouth went dry. Soon she would know.

Dalvik was beautiful. Green acres of land rolled down from forests of firs, where a smattering of wooden-framed houses scattered down to where the land flattened out to meet the wide expanse of the Tunnhovdf-jord. But the beauty of the place was of secondary importance just then. Nerves had started to bite.

But it was too late to have last-minute thoughts. Mr Pearson had stopped the car and, having asked Zarah the name of her aunt, he was enquiring of a passer-by if he knew where the Kildedalen residence was.

'*Mange takk*', Mr Pearson practised his Norwegian as he thanked the stranger. 'It's only two minutes away,' he told Zarah cheerfully as he re-started the car. A few minutes later, he had stopped the car again. 'This is it,' he pronounced, and suddenly Zarah's insides felt as though they did not belong to her.

The house was large, stood in its own grounds, and was a three-storied building. Its comparatively new construction reminded Zarah that her aunt had moved from her old address a couple of years before.

She was out of the car waiting while Mr Pearson extracted her suitcase from the boot, when it struck her that it would be the height of bad manners after their kindness, not to invite them to meet her aunt.

'You'll come in?' she suggested.

'You go along in and surprise your aunt,' Mr Pearson declined happily, and cut off her grateful thanks for the lift by bidding her, in chorus with his wife, 'have a terrific holiday.'

Zarah stood back and waved as they drove off. Then, feeling very much alone and in fear that she might give in to the impulse to chase after the Pearsons, she turned resolutely to face the house.

Each step forward, until she was confronted by the stout front door, had been an effort. She put her suitcase down, swallowed hard, and stretched out a shaky hand to the door bell.

An age seemed to elapse before she heard the firm tread of footsteps. Then the door opened, and the man who looked sternly down at her, when she was tall herself, appeared to be a giant. Big, blond, grey-eyed, and with an expression that was not at all welcoming, the man took in her dark hair, her slender shape, and the suitcase at her feet.

Unspeaking, he inclined his head to invite her to state

her business. Put off by his cool appraisal, when her
insides had enough to contend with, Zarah began, 'M-my
name ...' and halted as it dawned on her that he
probably didn't know one word of English. But, since she
didn't know a word of Norwegian, she pushed on, 'My
name is Zarah Thornton ...' Sshe got no further. Before
she could go on to explain that she had come to see her
aunt, the man's cool look had changed to one of total
fury.

'My God!' he exploded, obviously quite at home in her
language despite his faint trace of accent. 'You couldn't
get here fast enough, could you!'

Too taken aback for the moment to remember that
it was not him she wanted this conversation with, but
her aunt, she began again, 'I—d-didn't decide to come
until ...'

'Until you received a letter from your aunt's lawyers,'
he cut in. 'Nothing would have kept you in England
then,' he rapped, and went on to stun her utterly as he
roared, 'you couldn't find the time to come to her funeral,
but as soon as you received that letter ...!' Zarah barely
heard what other words of fury he rained down on her
head. Shocked, stunned, her brain had caught hold of the
only thing that had any relevance to it.

'My aunt's—*dead*?' she whispered. 'You're saying-
...Aunt Anne has died? That—I've come *too late*!'

'Anne Kildedalen died three weeks ago,' he retorted,
and it was clear from his sceptical look that he thought
she already knew that. His eyes flicked over Zarah's
night-black hair and perfect features. 'It's my guess, Miss
Thornton,' he said acidly, 'that when it's to your
advantage, you'd make a point of being early.' Oddly, as
though suspecting that someone else was about to join
them, he looked over his shoulder. Then, he instructed
curtly, 'You'd better come in.'

Still shaken by the realisation that even before she had found that marriage certificate, even before she had decided to come to Norway to find the truth, her aunt had died, Zarah was left to cope with her own luggage. She picked up her case, but, numbed as she was, it was only just starting to register that, with her aunt dead, there was every likelihood that the truth she sought might well have died with her!

CHAPTER TWO

ZARAH crossed the Kildedalen threshold and followed the furious Norwegian along a wide hall. She was still in shock when he abruptly halted at one of the doors and she bumped straight into him.

As if it was beneath him to touch her, he made no attempt to help her regain her balance, but left her to sort herself out. 'Drop your case there,' he grunted, and opened the door to instruct, 'wait in here.' Then swiftly, obviously not deigning to consider his command would not be obeyed, he turned on his heel and left her.

More because she felt the need at the moment for someone to give her some point of direction than to obey his curt order, Zarah entered what was a drawing room, to note distractedly that it was furnished very similarly to an English drawing room.

That was about all she had time to notice. Wherever he had been, the Norwegian's errand must have been a brief one, for he was soon back—his demeanour she saw, not improved with keeping. She decided to get in first.

'You said my aunt is dead?' she questioned, part of her still not ready to believe it.

'As I advised you in my letter,' he replied tersely, 'she died on the twenty-seventh of June.'

'*You* wrote to me?' Confusion joined her stunned feelings. She made an attempt to think more clearly, and saw it was immaterial who it was who had written. 'I didn't get any letter from you,' she told him.

His disbelief was evident when he scorned, 'You'll tell

20

me next that you haven't received a letter from your aunt's lawyer either!'

Zarah was tired, not a little defeated, and definitely in no mood for riddles. 'Look,' she said crossly, numbness and confusion mingling to make her voice tart, 'I've been travelling most of the day to get here. I'm ...'

'Naturally you'd make tracks for Dalvik the moment your plane touched down in Oslo,' he cut in.

'I didn't come by plane,' she snapped, 'I came by boat. I stayed overnight in Bergen.'

Since he seemed to think she had made all haste to get there, though not for her aunt's funeral, Zarah thought that might have knocked his scepticism for six. Fat chance, she discovered. All she had succeeded in doing was to give his obviously razor-sharp mind food for finding a reason why she had not got there jet-propelled.

'You have a fear of flying?' he charged abruptly.

'My father was killed in a flying accident ...' Suddenly she stopped. Damn this man, she thought, feeling foolish into the bargain, since it just wasn't rational that because her father had been killed in an aircrash—a father she had never known—she had grown up with a fear of flying. 'What if I have?' she flared, and found that being made to feel a fool had done wonders for her latent aggression. 'Who are you?' she erupted suddenly, her aggressiveness riding high when his only response was to stare coldly at the angry sparkle in her eyes, 'I want to see Herr Kildedalen,' she demanded, wondering belatedly why she had not demanded to see him before this. 'Or,' she challenged, the bit well and truly between her teeth now, 'is he dead too?'

The moment she had said the words, she regretted them. Not because the dark frown that came to the Norwegian's face bothered her but, because feeling emotionally drained, she knew her words had lacked her normal sensitivity. Not that the scowling Norwegian seemed to think that she had any sensitivity at all.

'For all the interest he's taking in life at this time in his bereavement,' he told her sharply, 'it's as though he has died with his wife.' A trace of something akin to worry briefly crossed his face, but it was coldly that he informed her, 'I'm Stein Kildedalen, his son,'

For a confused instant, Zarah wondered, if she was Anne's child—was Stein Kildedalen her half-brother? But in the next instant, observing that he appeared to be about thirty-five, she knew that could not be so. Anne was not old enough to have a son his age.

'I didn't know Herr Kildedalen had a son by his first marriage,' she muttered, and saw that the son of the house cared not one whit whether she had or had not known. What he did care about, though, was his father, for he lost no time in telling her bluntly:

'I'm here to ensure that no more stress is added to that which my father is already suffering.'

His message was clear, and Zarah did not like it—even is she had been a shade insensitive once. 'You think I intend to upset him,' she bridled.

'I've no idea how it will affect him to see a relative of the wife he adored,' he retorted. 'But he's in no condition to see anyone tonight.'

'He's—taking my aunt's death badly?'

'You could say that,' was the curt reply, and suddenly all Zarah's sensitivity rushed to the fore. She remembered her mother's death, and how she had not been able to talk about it. How she was not sure she could talk about it now, a month later. And, in truth, she was not sure what she wanted to say, or could or should say to Herr Kildedalen when she saw him. Which left her with very little she could say to his son either, except:

'How—I mean, my aunt. I didn't even know she was ill.'

'So *you* say,' Stein Kildedalen said brusquely, and with no expression of sympathy for the loss of her mother, he went on, 'It happened on the day your letter arrived telling her of her sister's death. Anne was out on an errand and must have had your news so much on her mind that, unthinkingly, she stepped out into fast-flowing traffic.'

'She was killed in a road traffic accident!'

'The driver tried to avoid her,' she was told flatly, 'but couldn't avoid hitting her.'

Zarah blanched at the picture his words conjured up. Bravely then, she ventured, 'You—your father—you blame me—my letter about my mother, for distracting my aunt and ultimately being the cause of her death?'

'Anne was terminally ill,' she was coldly advised. 'She was saved a more lingering and painful death—as my father was spared the agony of having to watch her die that way.'

Long moments of silence filled the room, broken by Zarah's gentle, 'Could—nothing be done?' For her pains, she was soundly rounded upon.

'God in heaven,' Stein Kildedalen exploded, 'do you think we didn't *try*? Do you think there wasn't a specialist, a quack, anyone who held out the least hope of a cure whom we didn't contact?'

'I'm sorry,' she apologised quickly, aware then that he too had been fond of her aunt. But her apology was abruptly brushed aside.

'Are you hungry?'

Zarah blinked. 'What?' she questioned blankly and learned that Stein Kildedalen did not suffer fools gladly.

'When did you last eat?'

'I'm not hungry, she gathered her scattered wits to tell

him, only to realise that the big Norwegian wasn't about
to coax her to partake at his father's table.

'Good,' he grunted, and went to the door opened it,
and hefted up her suitcase. 'I'll find you somewhere to
sleep,' he told her. 'Follow me.'

'But . . .' she started to protest. Had she nursed some
sketchy idea to say that in the circumstances she would
book into a hotel for the night, she soon discovered that
Stein Kildedalen thought she was protesting on a
different front. For he was his most disagreeable yet,
when he turned to snarl at her:

'You're not seeing my father tonight, and that's final! I
need time to tell him you're here. That time,' he added
heavily, 'is not now.'

Taken aback, Zarah could only say, 'Shall I see him
tomorrow?

'I'll see how he is tomorrow,' he replied shortly, and
headed for the stairs. Zarah followed him.

He lead the way to a large airy bedroom where he
dropped her suitcase to disappear briefly and appear
again carrying a light duvet, pillows, and all he thought
necessary for her overnight comfort. Then, to show he
thought he had done all he should, without a word of
good night, he left her.

Zarah almost crumpled when the door closed behind
him. She did not give way to tears, however. She was
tired, shaken, and not a little confused, but tears were no
solution.

Wearily she made up her bed, then unstrapped her
suitcase to extract toiletries and nightwear. Her mind
busy, she went to the adjoining bathroom to wash. She
was still chasing one thought after another when she
climbed into bed. Somehow she just could not accept that
this trip to Norway was going to end with her turning
right round and going back to England without ever

knowing whose daughter she was.

Her hopes lifted at the thought that perhaps Haldor Kildedalen knew the truth. But they were as suddenly dashed. According to Stein Kildedalen, his father had adored her aunt, and was grief-stricken at her passing. How could she intrude on that grief to question him? If he did not know, she might only set *him* questioning, and so possibly could cause him even greater harrowing grief.

A picture of Stein Kildedalen shot into her head, and she wished she had not thought of the wretched man. For, when she had better things to do than to remember that tall, broad-shouldered Norwegian with a rock-hard chin and eyes that glinted with ice, that picture refused to budge. Though why he was so against her, she could not fathom. And what on earth had he been going on about when he had spoken of not one, but two, letters she was supposed to have received from Norway?

Unable to see, either, why she should not have received those letters, she found herself unable to keep her eyes open any longer, and gave up trying to work out Stein Kildedalen's attitude towards her. Suddenly she had started to feel cosily warm and comfortable. Mentally fatigued, she fell asleep.

Someone knocking at her bedroom door aroused her the next morning, and she had just struggled to sit up when a short and plump woman entered.

'God morgen' the mature lady greeted her, and passed by the foot of the bed to put the tray she was carrying on a desk at the window.

'G-God morgen,' Zarah attempted, amazed to find it was daylight, and that she had just had her best night's sleep since her mother had died. 'I'm Zarah Thornton,' she halted the woman's progress as she went to leave. Then she realised that she had just come across the first person so far in this country who did not speak English.

'Frøken Zarah Thornton,' she tried, hoping to introduce herself that way.

She was successful: a smile of comprehension broke out, and the plump little lady pointed to herself. 'Fru Onsvag,' she said.

Zarah returned her smile, assuming that the lady might be the housekeeper, but since conversation of any sort was going to be all uphill, she sat smiling until the woman had left, then got out of bed to investigate the tray.

Removal of the covering cloth showed two things. One, that breakfast had been brought to her room. The other, that since, plainly, Stein Kildedalen did not want her to join him and his father at the breakfast table, he expected her to wait in her room until such time as he came to see her.

A spark of mutiny made her want to charge down to the breakfast room just to show him that, today, she was not going to take orders from him. But the mutinous thought faded under the memory of the mental pain his father was suffering. Kick against Stein Kildedalen and his high-handed authority though she might, he knew his father better than she, and she had to leave it to him to tell him she was there in the best way he thought fit. Then Zarah realised that she was starving.

Seated before a similar sort of breakfast to the one she had eaten yesterday, she gathered that this must be the typical type of Norwegian start to the day. There was plenty to choose from. Fresh white and brown bread lay on one plate, and a variety of cheese slices, cold meats and cold fish on other plates. There was even a tasty-looking pastry to finish off with, as well as orange juice and coffee.

Zarah was tucking into an open sandwich of cheese on bread and butter, when suddenly her gaze went to the truly magnificent view from the window. Spellbound, she gazed past the grounds of the Kildedalen home to the lush green meadows beyond. Past the meadows was a wide stretch of fjord, with a gigantic backdrop of mountains and forest and peaks, all reflected in mirror image in the clear and pure waters of the fjord.

How long she sat totally entranced, she had no idea. Ever since she had found that marriage certificate, the moment she awoke her brain would be on the fidget. But she suddenly came to, to realise incredibly that for the first time in an age, she had spent a good while without one agitating thought there in her head to trouble her.

Having eaten all she wanted, Zarah left her chair before the view should again hypnotise her. Quickly she went to bathe and dress. She had enjoyed her moments of peace, and wanted more. But she had no idea when Stein Kildedalen would arrive, and she had no wish to still be in her nightclothes when he came. He had no good opinion of her now, and she knew that, if she knew nothing else. And while she cared not a jot for his good opinion, today she felt more herself, and knew that sparks would soon fly if he caught her looking as if she'd just got out of bed, and looked down his superior nose as if to say 'Lazy slob!'

As luck would have it, she had just finished running a comb through her shoulder-length black-hair when a knock on her door told her she had company. It could be Fru Onsvag come to collect her used breakfast dishes, but since that good lady had entered following her knock, Zarah decided that it must be Stein Kildedalen. She went and opened the door.

His size had been no figment of an overtired imagination, she saw, for he appeared to fill the doorway. 'Good morning,' she attempted a totally wasted civilised greeting.

'Come,' was all he answered, and without obvious speed, but with a speed that obliged her to put on a spurt to draw level with him, he turned and went to the stairhead.

'You've told your father I'm here?' she asked, and had to hold back on the urge to find out how much strength she would need to push the arrogant brute down the stairs, when he totally ignored her question.

She determined then that not one more word would she say to him than she had to, and concentrated instead on keeping up with him. Down the wide staircase they went, to take a right turn at the bottom, and along another part of the hall, until, without so much as sparing her a glance, Stein Kildedalen stopped at one of the doors and pushed it open.

She did not thank him when, possibly because certain politenesses were bred in him, he stood back to allow her to go into the room first.

The room was much smaller than the drawing room he had taken her to last night. It was a comfortable room, a homely room and, she guessed, a favourite room.

A white-haired elderly man sat hunched over in an easy chair. Zarah went forward, but Stein, his expression warning her she would be in trouble if she upset the old man, was there before her. Haldor Kildedalen made an attempt to rise when Stein made the introductions, but as she stretched out her hand, Zarah quickly slipped into the chair that was placed near him.

It seemed to her, as Haldor Kildedalen gripped her hand tightly, as though he was in need of someone else's strength to see him through the day. 'I'm sorry to have arrived at such a dreadful time,' she said gently, her heart going out to the grief-worn man. He had the same grey eyes as his son, but where Stein's eyes were alert and alive, there was a look in his father's eyes of a man who was dead inside. She saw an exhausted tiredness in them, which suggested he had not slept very much since the death of his wife.

His red-rimmed eyes fell to the hand he still had in his grip, and he loosened his clasp. 'I'm—sorry too,' he said slowly, but as his hand fell back into his lap, his eyes stayed on her, and to her surprise, he asked, 'you will stay with us?' Zarah hesitated. She had thought she might be heading back to Bergen once this introduction was over. 'Please,' he said, seeing her hesitation, 'I should like you to stay in my home.'

He seemed to sincerely want her to have a holiday in his home, she thought, as she realised that her plans had not yet been fully formulated in her head. But, her own plans aside, her heart-strings were pulled by this dreadfully saddened man. Suddenly she just knew that if it would please him; if it would give him any kind of tiny solace to have a blood relation of his wife in his home in this time of his greatest personal tragedy, then she would stay.

A flicked glance to Stein showed her that he was watching her with steely-eyed thoroughness. One wrong word from her, and she just knew she would be yanked out of there before she could blink. She ignored him.

'If you would like me to stay,' she smiled at Haldor Kildedalen, 'then I should like very much to stay—for a little while.'

The white-haired man did not return her smile, and she guessed it would be a long while before he would smile again. She had the impression, though, just before he rested his head back, that he was pleased she had accepted his invitation.

Not so his son. If Zarah had seen that the senior Kildedalen was for the moment worn out, then so had

Stein. Before she could make some excuse to leave the room, he had beaten her to it.

'I have something to discuss with Zarah,' he told his father. 'I'll come back later.'

Zarah was still recovering from the astonishment of realising that Stein Kildedalen had actually deigned to use her first name, when he escorted her from the small sitting-room. He had taken her to the drawing-room she had briefly visited the previous evening when it dawned on her that, in his concern for his father, he would be on first-name terms with the devil himself if it would guard his parent from any undercurrent of animosity which he did not need.

There was no time, however, for her to ponder on the 'something' Stein had said he wanted to discuss with her. For no sooner was the drawing room closed than—far away from his father's hearing—Stein's animosity returned in full flow.

'How kind of you to agree to stay,' he opened, not attempting to suggest she be seated, but content to offer his sarcastic comments while they stood facing each other across the carpet.

Zarah still had no clue to why this man should be so aggressive with her, but she held on to her temper, and pushed out a phoney smile. 'I thought it would please you,' she told him pleasantly. 'Since I shall be here for only a short while, though, I've every confidence we shall be able to keep out of each other's way.'

'Short while!' he gritted, in disgust. 'It'll be the longest six months I've ever lived through!'

'Six months!' she exclaimed, feeling as though she had just come into a movie halfway through. 'What the dickens are you talking about? I've agreed to . . .'

'We're alone,' he severed through her attempt to tell him that she had agreed to stay a week—a fortnight at the most. 'There's no need to put on an act with me.'

'I'm not acting!' she flared, her hot protest ignored, when he continued:

'You know damn well you've not the smallest intention of risking your inheritance by leaving Norway a day under the six months stipulated.'

Zarah's mouth opened. Several words came to her tongue, but the one that emerged was a staggered, 'In— heritance?'

'I said cut the acting,' he grated. 'Langaard wouldn't write to you stating how Anne had left you all her shares in Kildedalen Industrier, and miss out "but only on condition that you spend six unbroken months in Norway".'

Zarah's mouth did not merely open, her jaw dropped. 'I ... It ...' she spluttered, and tried again. 'I didn't receive any lett ... Who's Langaard?'

His cynicism that she had never heard of anyone called Langaard was visible in the contemptuous look Stein threw her. 'Olav Langaard, as you well know,' he said tautly, 'is the lawyer whom your aunt, and my father, retained when they semi-retired to Dalvik two years ago.'

'But ...'

'Your aunt's errand on the day she was killed,' he went on as if she had not spoken, 'was to visit Langaard for the purpose of changing her will in your favour. You, Miss Thornton,' he said grimly, taking no account of how her eyes were growing wider and wider, 'stand to be a very wealthy woman.'

His statement that she stood to be a very wealthy woman had little impact. What did shake Zarah, though, was the implication that rushed in from the whole of what he had just said. For it showed clearly that Anne, the aunt who had not seen her since she was a year old, must have cared for her. Zarah knew she needed time to get it all sorted out in her head, but considering she had thought she might never know the truth, suddenly she had the very definite feeling that she might be much nearer than she had realised to finding out what she needed to know.

She flicked a glance at the hostile son of the house, but knew from his warring expression that to approach him with any of the questions in her head would be a waste of time. She doubted he could tell her any of what she wanted to know anyway. Olav Langaard, though, her thoughts sped on, as her aunt's lawyer, had surely been in her confidence. He would be the one to tell her everything that there was to know.

Her mouth dry from the sudden feeling that the answers she wanted might be within her grasp, Zarah addressed Stein carefully. 'I think,' she said, 'that I should like to see this Mr Langaard.'

'Now whatever made me think that could well be your first action today?' Stein offered sarcastically. Woodenly, Zarah refused to bite, then found she was not going to have to wait very much longer to know everything when, as he strode to the door, the interview over as far as he was concerned, Stein Kildedalen informed her, 'You've an appointment to see Langaard this afternoon.'

Zarah spent the rest of the morning in her room. She busied herself unpacking her suitcase, her mind as busy as her hands. Stein, believing that she was there in response to some letter from Olav Langaard, must have made that appointment for her that morning, she realised. At any other time it might have rankled that he thought she was straining at the leash to see the solicitor in order to know all the ins and outs of her inheritance. But she was too busy with trying to remember what else Stein had told her.

Emotion smote her as she recalled that on the very

morning Anne had received the news of Margaret's death, Anne, knowing she was terminally ill herself, had gone out on an errand. That errand, as Zarah now knew, had been to see a solicitor.

Emotion threatening to cloud her thinking, Zarah tried to think logically. That logical thinking took her back to the trust fund which Grandfather Gentry had set up for her mother. Grandfather Gentry was said to have been a fair and a lovable man, and try as she might, Zarah just could not see any fair-minded man investing in a trust fund for one of his daughters and not the other. It naturally followed that Anne had known where Margaret's income had come from, and how it would cease when Margaret died. Which just had to mean that Anne, aware that her own time was limited, had, by leaving those shares the way she had, wanted to ensure that her niece would be well provided for.

Zarah was uncertain if she could draw from Anne's action any assumption that she was a closer relation to her than a niece. But, her stomach churning, whether from apprehension or excitement she knew not, all she knew was that her visit to the solicitor this afternoon could well give her all the answers.

Fru Onsvag came in just then to sign to her that lunch was ready, so Zarah went off with her to the dining-room.

Both Stein Kildedalen and his father were there, but when Stein stood until she was seated, she guessed it was more because he did not want his father to know that they would be at each other's throats, given half a chance, than from any wish to show her courtesy.

'You have been out this morning?' Haldor Kildedalen asked, and from where Zarah was sitting he looked so dreadfully spent, she thought it an effort for him to raise his head.

'I used the morning to unpack,' she replied, but as she caught Stein's dark look on her, and saw from his scowl that he was not at all thrilled to hear she was bedding herself in, she could not resist tacking on, 'I've ample time to take a look around.'

She fielded his grim look, and as the meal progressed, with his father eating very little and appearing to be in some other world, she fell to wondering how much either of them knew. The state Haldor was in, she knew she could not ask him. Stein, though . . .

A moment later she realised, positively, that he knew nothing. If Stein Kildedalen, crushingly blunt, had so much as an inkling of what she suspected, whether or not she was completely ignorant that her aunt could well have been her mother, he would by now have bluntly brought it out into the open.

Her thoughts against him were all at once rebellious, and she was about to ask sarcastically, since he knew how keen she was to get to the solicitors, if he would mind telling her where Olav Langaard's office was, when suddenly she remembered his father was there. How, when he was suffering so badly, could she even breathe the word solicitor in his presence? The memory must be painfully clear, without her reminding him, that his wife had been coming away from the lawyer's office when that accident had occurred.

The meal was almost at an end when Zarah began to grow anxious. Then she started to dislike Stein Kildedalen more intensely. Who did he think he was, the lofty swine, to tell her out of the blue that she had appointment with the solicitor that afternoon, and then stride off? She had no idea of the time of her appointment, and no clue to where the solicitor's offices were. Dalvik appeared to be no more than a village. Olav Langaard could have his offices miles away!

She had begun to feel anxious, now the carrot of the appointment had been dangled, that she might miss it altogether, when she heard Haldor Kildedalen address his son in Norwegian. Instantly he caught her eyes on him, though, and he was apologising.

'I'm sorry, Zarah,' he said, 'I forgot—I was just asking Stein about your appointment with Langaard. He tells me you are to see him this afternoon.'

'That's right,' she agreed quietly, but she felt sensitive about saying any more on the subject.

'You will drive Zarah to keep her appointment?' Haldor Kildedalen addressed his son, and added, 'I shall not come to harm if left alone for a few hours.'

From that, Zarah guessed that Stein feared for his father's safety when he was not there, and quickly she butted in, to state, 'I'm sure, if—Stein—tells me where Herr Langaard is, and how to get there, that I can find my own way.'

'Stein will take you,' Haldor Kildedalen insisted. 'Won't you?' he asked him.

'I shouldn't dream of letting Zarah go to the lawyers on her own,' Stein replied with a smile, and suddenly Zarah was wary.

Somehow she had the very definite feeling that Stein Kildedalen, forced as he was by his parent to chauffeur her to the solicitors, did not intend to leave her outside Mr Langaard's office. All at once she had the feeling that Stein was just not the type of person to be left cooling his heels while she did her business with the legal representative. When she had so much to ask Mr Langaard which she regarded as highly confidential, she had the ominous feeling that Stein Kildedalen fully intended to sit in—on her entire interview!

CHAPTER THREE

'WHERE are we going?' Zarah thought she should ask as early in the afternoon she sat beside Stein Kildedalen in his sleek black car.

His impatient look reminded her that she was supposed to know Olav Langaard's office address from the letter he had sent. But, 'Geilo,' Stein said shortly.

'That far?'

Her question went unanswered, and something very impolite rose to her lips. She swallowed it. She must try to remain polite. If she was to find some tact to tell him— politely in front of the solicitor—that he could wait outside, then politeness and tact would be easier if the drive was accomplished without them going at it hammer and tongs.

She had not expected him to engage her in pleasantries during the drive, so she could not say she was disappointed that he volunteered not one word of conversation. She concentrated on the view, which, since it was absolutely breathtaking, was no hardship. After some while, however, she found she had the ability to admire scenery while at the same time her brain could plague her with yet more questions.

Why, when her mother had kept nothing else in the way of private papers, had she left that marriage certificate for her to find? Had she merely forgotten about it? Had ... Suddenly Zarah remembered again how her mother had once said 'You've a fine brain', and she started to wonder: had her mother intended she should use her brain in this instance? Had she meant all along to tell her the truth but, because of some emotional block or other, been unable to bring herself to tell her? Or was it simply that there was no reason for her to hide that marriage certificate, because a genuine mistake about the names had been made a second time? If that was true, though, it still left the information about her mother being a sales assistant as incorrect, not to mention the wrong statement of her age.

Zarah left the tangle of her thoughts and pinned her hopes on the lawyer being able to clear everything up. If he was in her aunt's confidence, soon she would know all there was to know.

She tried to give all her attention to the panorama, but her nerves were under attack from what she might shortly learn. The stony silence from the man sitting next to her suddenly got to her, and the next moment words were bursting from her.

'You said this morning that your father and my aunt semi-retired to Dalvik two years ago.' He made no answer, and in spite of herself, Zarah was needled by his determination to ignore her whenever possible. 'Do you think,' she persisted, as determined to get a word from him as he seemed set on not answering, 'that your father will take more of an interest in the business now that my aunt . . .?'

'What's the matter—afraid I'm not as good at the helm as he was?' Stein put in. 'Are you fearful your shares in Kildedalen Industrier might go crashing down?'

'You're impossible!' Zarah exploded, then wished she had stayed silent. Ten seconds later, though, she had cooled down, and her brain cogs had again gone into action. 'So, you're in charge of Kildedalen Industrier?'

He really was the most infuriating man! Had she not been looking at him, she would have missed the nod of his head which confirmed that he was the man in charge.

More seconds ticked by, then recalling, without much interest, that Stein had said she stood to be a wealthy woman, she found her curiosity stirring.

'What exactly do Kildedalen Industrier do?' she asked.

He threw her a long-suffering look which she took to mean that he wished she would shut up. She then wished she had. Because after telling her briefly, 'We're producers and exporters of metals,' deliberately to make her eyes glaze over, she felt sure, he went into a welter of technical detail. Had her head not been swimming by the end of it, Zarah rather thought she ought to know quite something about silicon, ferrosilicon, magnesium, and aluminium. 'Of course,' he concluded, casting a self-satisfied look at her blank expression, 'we're for ever on the lookout for a way to produce more refined metals.'

'Of course,' she murmured, feeling the greatest urge to hit that smug look off his face. But, since nice girls did not go around giving way to such impulses, all she added was a restrained, 'Thank you, that was most interesting.'

'My pleasure,' he drawled.

Silenced for a while, Zarah nevertheless soon found another question on the end of her tongue. 'You—um—you don't keep charge of Kildedalen Industrier from Dalvik, though, do you?'

His appearance of being pleased to have at last shut her up promptly vanished. 'If you're asking do I reside in Dalvik with my father and . . .' he broke off, and she guessed he always thought of his father and Anne as one unit.

'I . . .' she got as far as saying quietly, but any softening in her was quickly banished when, with the habit he had of cutting off anything he did not want to hear, he did it again.

'For your information, I have my own home on the Sognefjord,' he told her.

'I'm not . . .'

'Plus another home in the north.'

'I couldn't care l. . .'

'And an apartment in Stavanger.'

'Anywhere else?' she shot in before he could cut her off.

'But,' he ignored her question, 'to answer what lies at the back of your question, I have no intention of leaving Dalvik for the present.'

'You—haven't?' she queried, any pleasure she might have found to be in beautiful Dalvik gone up in smoke.

'I've taken leave from my work to be near to my father,' Stein went on relentlessly. 'I shall stay with him, *in Dalvik*, for as long as it takes for his depression to clear.' An insincere smile suddenly appeared on his well shaped mouth, when he added pleasantly, 'Believe me, Miss Thornton, if it takes six months for my father's health to improve, then I shall not leave Dalvik until those six months are up.'

As none-too-subtle hints went, that topped the lot. As plainly as if he had just said it, Zarah saw that Stein Kildedalen had just told her that his father was not the only one he was going to keep his eye on while he was in Dalvik.

'As long as your work doesn't suffer,' she said sweetly, knowing in her bones that there was no way she was going to stay in the same house, or the same village as him, for six months.

'Once my holiday period is over, I can well make Dalvik my working base,' Stein told her.

'Super,' she smiled, and kept on smiling as she told him falsely, 'it looks as if we're going to see quite a lot of each other.'

Her smile, in conjunction with his, slipped. Briefly they exchanged glares. In mutually grim silence, they travelled the rest of the way to Geilo.

Herr Langaard was a tall spare man in his late fifties. He came out of his office to greet them, where Stein's innate courtesy returned for long enough for him to introduce his father'sEnglish guest.

'How do you do,' Zarah said politely, shaking hands with the lawyer, while she searched for some polite way to tell Stein to clear off.

'I'm sorry your visit to Norway had to be in such sad circumstances,' murmured the lawyer.

'Zarah is bearing up very bravely,' Stein stretched her growing urge to hit him to extremes.

'We all have our crosses to bear,' she smiled sadly up into his face, but he was the only one to see the sparks that flashed in her eyes.

'You'll forgive me if I leave you with Herr Langaard for half an hour?' Stein asked her, and in her relief that he was making himself scarce, she was able to ignore the aggression that lurked in his eyes. 'I've a small matter to attend to while I'm in Geilo.'

'I'll see you shortly,' she replied, and for Olav Langaard's benefit, she smiled prettily at Stein, then turned to go with the lawyer into his inner sanctum.

'Firstly,' began Herr Langaard, ushering her to a chair, his English as good as that of many of his countrymen, 'I must apologise for the delay in writing to you.' Zarah refrained from telling him that up until a few days ago, no notification from him had been received in England. She could not deny a feeling of wishing Stein Kildedalen was there to hear, though, when he went on to explain how, wishing to accommodate his staff as far as possible when they all appeared to want to take their main holiday at the same time, it had left him very short-handed. 'That is why I am working on a Saturday afternoon,' he sent her a charming if toothy smile. 'But you are here now, and I can explain details to you in much greater depth. I suspect, though, that Herr Kildedalen has already informed you of your inheritance.'

'It was Stein, actually,' she said, nerves starting to nibble as she endeavoured to let the solicitor know that she was more interested in hearing more about her aunt than her will. 'He has explained fully about the business and the shares,' she added with a smile.

Then she promptly forgot about Stein, but as Olav Langaard insisted on telling her all about her aunt's will, she learned not one word of what else her aunt had confided in him.

He had just finished outlining how, in order to claim her inheritance, she must not leave Norway for so much as one day during the next six months, when Zarah saw she would have to pretend that she and her aunt were on much closer terms than they had been.

'My—aunt,' she deliberately hesitated before the word 'aunt', her eyes watching his for any give-away sign, 'really loved Norway. She must have wanted me to learn to love her adopted country as much as she did.'

'I believe she was very happy here,' he commented, which to Zarah's mind gave away absolutely nothing.

'She never returned to England,' she pressed on, and, exaggerating the 'Thank you' letters she had penned, 'naturally, we corresponded frequently.'

'Naturally,' he agreed.

Beset by a feeling of being bogged down and getting nowhere, somehow Zarah felt it was like a betrayal of both her mother and her aunt, and also, to some extent, Haldor Kildedalen, to come straight out and ask point blank if she was Anne Kildedalen's daughter. Which left her to search up other avenues.

'Even so,' she said slowly, her thoughts on the stipulation that she should stay in Norway for six months, 'it was something of a surprise to learn that Fru Kildedalen had left her will the way she had.'

The serious expression that came over the lawyer's face sent her nerves nipping harder. Had she hoped, though, that he was about to reveal matters of a more personal nature, Zarah was left more baffled than enlightened when he questioned:

'Because of the take-over bid for Kildedalen Industrier last year?'

Fighting her way through the fog, she quickly realised that her statement that Stein had explained fully about the business must have given Herr Langaard the notion that she knew far more than she did. That statement, coupled with Stein's outward show of being friendly towards her when he had introduced her, must have given Olav Langaard the idea that there was little she did not know concerning the business.

With no wish to have the lawyer go cold on her at this stage, Zarah saw she could not disabuse him, and that there was nothing for it but to play it by ear. The conversation she'd had with Stein on the way to Geilo came in handy.

'Stein's still in charge, though,' she said brightly, and hung on to her smile when the lawyer replied:

'Thanks to Fru Kildedalen's shares swaying the vote on his side. Which was only fair, since it is thanks to Stein Kildedalen and his endeavours that Kildedalen Industrier ceased to struggle for existence and is today one of the most profitable metal-producing companies in Norway. The shares,' he added, 'are rising daily in value.'

It was news that Stein Kildedalen, and not his father,

was the one responsible for the company being the huge success it was. To hear the lawyer tell it, Haldor Kildedalen had had no hand in its success. Zarah felt curiosity stir, but more particularly, she wanted to get the conversation back to her aunt.

'It was lucky my—aunt—had those shares to vote with,' she opined. 'Though I'm sure she would not have dreamt of voting any other way.'

Olav Langaard nodded his balding head in agreement, and Zarah just knew that she was going to get nothing out of him—not unless she gave him a little information first. But the best she could come up with was information she guessed he must, as her aunt's legal representative, already know.

'Aunt Anne must have purchased those shares at the start when the price was low,' she said, and rushed on, her tone confiding, 'my aunt had money of her own from a trust fund set up by her father.'

There, she thought, surely, since he knew she was privy to that, he would be more forthcoming. She waited, but only to discover that her assumption that her aunt had paid for her shares from her own money was wrong.

'Fru Kildedalen did not purchase her shares,' she was solemnly informed.

'She didn't?'

'They were a gift from her husband.'

'Oh!' exclaimed Zarah, her head starting to buzz with fresh questions. Fresh questions which would detract from what she really wanted to know, if she voiced them. She hesitated and, momentarily stumped, filled the pause with what was, for her, a throw-away question. 'Are you sure?' she asked.

'I am certain,' the lawyer replied. 'Only three weeks ago Fru Kildedalen sat where you are now, and discussed her shares fully. She told me then that her husband gave the firm up into his son's keeping some eight years ago. Subsequently, when four years afterwards Herr Stein Kildedalen had the company—er—on its feet, and he floated the company, he made his father a gift of a great number of shares. Your aunt and her husband were as one,' he explained kindly. 'It therefore followed, automatically in Herr Haldor Kildedalen's mind, that what was his was his wife's. He immediately signed half of his shares over to her name.'

As Zarah quickly grasped that information, she just had to ask, 'Stein K . . . he'd know what his father would do with half of his gift?'

'Of course,' came the unhesitating reply.

'Just as he would know that—er—when the crunch came, that is, if someone should try to take over Kildedalen Industrier, my aunt would vote whichever way her husband voted?'

'It would be a foregone conclusion,' he confirmed. 'Just,' he added, peering over the top of his spectacles as if to gauge her reaction, 'as he will know that, should there be another amibitious take-over bid, you will vote with your shares, on his side.'

He was awaiting her reply, Zarah knew that. But, since he was giving away nothing of what was of more prime importance to her, she told him quickly, 'I wouldn't do anything else,' and then took the bull by the horns, to ask him directly, 'Did Fru Kildedalen say anything more? I mean, did she confide anything of a—personal nature—about me?'

'Fru Kildedalen was most anxious to have everything signed and witnessed before she left my office that day,' he said after a few moments spent in thinking back. 'But, apart from making sure we had your name spelled correctly, and assuring herself that there could be no mistake about her wishes, she said nothing that related personally to you.'

That, Zarah saw, must be that. Herr Langaard could not have told her more clearly that if Anne Kildedalen did have a secret to confide, she certainly had not confided that secret to him. She knew that her appointment with him was just about over. Yet there was still something in her which refused to let her get up and leave it there.

'Had you known Fru Kildedalen for very long?' she remained seated to ask.

'For a few years,' he replied, appearing in no hurry for her to go.

'But—my aunt—she never spoke of me, until her last visit?'

'I did not know she had a niece in England until then,' he told her.

Zarah pushed out another smile. 'I wasn't prying for you to break a confidence,' she excused her question. 'It's just that with my aunt leaving me so much, it has all been something of a shock.'

The lawyer returned her smile. 'There are no confidences to break,' he replied. 'I have told you everything there is to tell you.' Zarah effectively hid her expression by getting to her feet. 'All you have to remember,' Herr Langaard went on as he stepped round his desk and escorted her to the door, 'is that if you leave Norway in under six months, those shares will revert to Herr Haldor Kildedalen.'

He went with her into the outer office, where Zarah saw that Stein had returned. There was a general shaking of hands, then the lawyer suggested:

'You will come to see me, with your passport, in six months' time, Miss Thornton.' He turned to Stein, to suggest, 'Perhaps you will escort her, Herr Kildedalen,' and with a genial look, 'who better to confirm that Miss Thornton has not left Norway during that time?'

Stein Kildedalen was in no more a talkative frame of mind driving back to Dalvik than he had been on the outward journey. This time, though, Zarah had no wish to force any sort of a conversation. Her nerves, her tension about the visit to Olav Langaard, had all been for nothing. She had learned nothing, because, plainly, he knew nothing.

Yet still the restless questioning persisted, and Zarah just knew that until she found out definitely, she was not going to have any peace from that one question which was beginning to haunt her. Whose daughter was she?

In what she knew before she began was a futile attempt, she checked over her conversation with Herr Langaard to see if there was anything she had missed.

Oblivious to Stein, she went over every word, look and nuance. Olav Langaard had been thorough in the way he had given her a detailed account of the shares she had inherited, but it was not the shares she was interested in. Although, now she came to think of it, she had learned more about Stein Kildedalen then she had about her aunt. To hear the lawyer tell it, Stein Kildedalen had laboured hard and long to get the firm where it was today. Well, good luck to him; she wasn't interested in his hard work, or his blatant hostility either.

She ejected Stein Kildedalen and his uncalled-for hostility from her mind, and again started to concentrate on what Herr Langaard had said about her aunt. Then, like a bolt from the blue, she remembered something the lawyer had said which she had not paid much attention to at the time. And, staggered, she suddenly knew exactly why Stein Kildedalen was so hostile towards her. For as she recalled the lawyer's view that, should there be another take-over bid Stein would know that she would vote her shares on his side, she realised that Stein believed nothing of the kind! As far as he was concerned, when it came to foregone conclusions, his only conclusion was that she would back the highest bidder!

He had made no bones about letting her know his opinion that it was only the scent of money that had brought her to Norway in the first place. He certainly had not believed her when she had said she had received neither his letter nor a letter from Herr Langaard. Stein Kildedalen's disgust that, while she had seen no need to attend her aunt's funeral, she had not been able to get to Dalvik fast enough when she had heard about those shares, had been all too evident.

Impulsively Zarah turned to him and almost blurted out a reiteration that she had not received any letter from Norway, and that he could check with Olav Langaard about the one he was supposed to have sent, if he did not believe her. But, noting her sudden movement, Stein had taken his eyes from the road to look at her, and the superior ice-cold glint in his eyes froze the words in her throat.

She turned back to face the front, realising that she would do better to get it all sorted out in her head first. She must not do anything on impulse. Danger lay that way, for she could easily find she had revealed the true reason for her visit to Norway, and that she must not reveal—to him.

Without a shadow of a doubt, Zarah knew that his protection of his father was such that just the merest suggestion that her quest might further upset him would see Stein throwing her out. He would have the doors locked and bolted after her without thinking twice, she just knew it. Strangely, when that should not have bothered her, Zarah found that it did.

But she had sufficient to think about without

searching into what feelings of security she must have found in Haldor Kildedalen's home. Her thoughts went back to her aunt's shares. Those shares which had originated from Stein and which, surely, he must have fully expected to revert to him one day.

Oh grief, she thought, fastening on the fact that it had been her aunt's shares which had once saved Stein from losing his firm. It must have knocked him sideways to learn that those shares had been willed out of the family!

No wonder he was so against her! With his opinion of her so low, all he could see was that, through her, he could easily be on the way to saying goodbye to the firm he had laboured so hard for!

CHAPTER FOUR

ZARAH was not sure if she had yet come to terms with her discovery of why Stein Kildedalen disliked her so intensely. None-the-less, as she dressed for dinner that night, she instinctively knew that no one was going to look down on her, no matter what they mistakenly believed.

The full-length mirror reflected an image of a tall, slender and elegant female, with dark shiny hair. Her white polka-dotted navy dress was deceptively simple and, to all but the most discerning eye, belied its expensive price tag. But Zara felt good in the dress and, her confidence still shaken, she *needed* to feel good.

The fact that it would please Stein Kildedalen never to see her again had hardly been veiled when he had pulled up outside the house. His none too subtle hint behind the curt, 'Dinner's at eight,' told her clearly that—since he must see her again—the evening meal time would be soon enough.

Not wanting his company either, she had gone straight to her room. Her head had been filled with a jumble of thoughts ever since.

Surely, when it was plain that Anne and Haldor had known a special kind of love, Anne must have had some love for her too. She must have done, to have done what she had with those shares her beloved husband had given her.

But was it a mother's love? Anne had left for Norway when Zarah was in hospital and year old, so her hospitalisation would have precluded any chance of a natural bonding. But had it been a natural mother's love which had seen Anne go against what her dear husband must have fully expected, and leave those shares away from his family?

Zarah had come to no certain judgement when she joined Haldor Kildedalen and his son in the dining-room. *'God kveld,'* she offered as, hoping the senior Kildedalen would forgive her phrase-book accent, she took the seat she had occupied at lunch time.

'Good evening,' Haldor Kildedalen replied courteous-ly to her greeting in English.

He had little else to say to her, though, and again he ate very little, so that Zarah began to think it was only his inbred courtesy to a guest that had seen him come to the table at all.

She had just eaten the last of her pork with creamed mushroom sauce, however, when, since she had to look somewhere, her glance fell on Stein. He was oblivious to her, she saw, but the look of concern on his face sent her gaze following his to see that his father, with an agony of pain in his expression, was looking at no one but her!

Choked by the welter of pain she observed in his red-rimmed eyes, Zarah was unable to say a word. Then Haldor Kildedalen caught her eyes on him, and, when she had thought he had forgotten all about her appointment with the solicitor that afternoon, he had collected himself to ask:

'Your meeting with Langaard was satisfactory, Zarah?'

From her point of view it had been far from satisfactory, but since he knew nothing of why she had wanted to see the lawyer, 'Yes, thank you, Herr Kildedalen,' she told him. She then knew that whatever his son thought of her, Haldor Kildedalen did not hold it against her that the shares had been willed out of the family. For, although it was hesitantly put, it was sincerely that he said:

'It would—please me—Zarah, if you would call me—hmm—perhaps—hmm—Uncle Haldor.'

Warmed by his invitation, although he was not up to smiling yet, 'I should like very much to call you Uncle Haldor,' Zarah answered gently, and despite a glimpse of a cold look from Stein, she smiled.

'Good,' said her new Uncle Haldor, but he had nothing more to say, nor did he have anything more to eat. As soon as the last course was over, he rose from his chair, bade her good-night and, Stein going with him, left the room.

She suspected they had gone to the small sitting-room which Stein had taken her to that morning. That room she had dubbed as private, and knew she would never enter it again unless invited. She rather thought Stein would stay with his father and guessed she would see neither of them again until the morning.

Zarah left the dining-room, but found she had a definite aversion to going back upstairs and to have to remain there to await breakfast time. Since the small and homely sitting-room was out of bounds, though, she decided that the drawing-room was the next best place to while away time until she felt like going to bed.

As ever, solitude gave her all the space she needed to have one thought after another jump into her head. If Haldor Kildedalen asking her to call him Uncle had started to make her feel less of an outsider, though, there was a restlessness in her as she remembered Stein's cold-eyed look on her. Unable to settle, she went to study an oil painting on a far wall with some vague notion of telling Stein Kildedalen that, whatever he might think of her, the firm of Kildedalen Industrier was as safe now as it had been while her aunt had been alive.

She had not decided just how she was going to tell him when suddenly the sound of firm footsteps nearing the drawing-room sent her impulsively darting over to the door.

'Stein!' she called quickly as she saw him. But when he did not falter in his stride but joined her in the drawing-room, she knew he had been making for that room anyway. The killing look he gave her for daring to use his first name, though, was all that was needed to send every other impulsive utterance from her mind.

When, with another of his none too subtle hints, he said curtly, 'I thought you'd gone to bed,' she knew that had he known she was in the drawing-room, he would have chosen somewhere else to take his ease.

That knowledge alone sent any remnant of wanting to tell him anything on its way. But then, with no intention of saying a word to him about the shares, before she could stop herself, she snapped:

'You know what thought did!'

Stein Kildedalen glowering at her was something she was getting used to. But as she weathered his grim silence that spoke of him not being particularly interested in hearing why she had called his name to attract his attention, so, startlingly, a new idea suddenly shot into her head. The idea took rapid growth, and all at once she had forgotten how much this man irked her. Because, with a sudden clarity of vision, Zarah had seen that in names—or to be more exact, the name her aunt had used when she had first come to Norway—lay the key to what she was there to find out!

Wondering why she had not hit upon this solution earlier, Zarah at the same time realised that it would be folly to come straight out and ask Stein if he had addressed Anne as Miss Gentry or as *Mrs Thornton*, before she had married his father.

'Did—er . . .' Nerves at his uninviting expression made her start off badly, and Zarah halted. Then, a trace belligerently she had to own, she adopted some of his bluntness, and asked, 'I expect my aunt had to housekeep for you too, in those early days before she married your father?'

Her question was all too obviously one he had not been expecting. But, save for a 'not that it's got anything to do with you' look, Stein, as if to find out what she was up to now, did reply. Terse though that reply was.

'I was living with my mother when Anne arrived from England.'

'Oh!' Zara exclaimed, feeling defeated before she had begun. Tenacity, however, took hold when she sensed that if she let this conversation go, she might never get another chance. Not without Stein suspecting that there was something deeper behind her questioning anyhow. 'But they had you to live with them before they were married?' she probed.

'After,' he said shortly, the narrowing of his eyes telling her that he had already started to object to her questions.

Expecting a rebuff any second, she jumped in before he could cut her down to size. 'From what I've gathered, Aunt Anne and your father enjoyed a marriage which was perfect.' Zarah admitted she felt edgy with him, and had to own to again being insensitive when, not without a trace of acid, she added, 'I'd have thought, with such a perfect married life, that they'd no need of a fifteen-year-old third.'

Her insensitivity had needled him, she could see it had before he barked harshly, 'I was fourteen, and *my life* was far from perfect!'

Immediately she was ashamed. How could she have let him goad her in to showing such insensitivity? 'Your father wanted you with him?' she asked quietly, and saw pride in Stein when, to let her know that Anne had not been pressured into giving him a home, he snapped:

'It was at Anne's suggestion I joined them. It was her opinion that my life might be happier with them than with a woman who cared more for a good time than she cared for my welfare.'

From the sound of it, his childhood had been no bed of roses. Zarah remembered her own childhood, the love she had received, and how cared for she had always been. And, 'You had it—rough?' she queried sympathetically—only to find he had no need of her sympathy.

'Mind your own damned business!' he grated stingingly.

The softening in her at the contrast in their different upbringings abruptly vanished. 'My apologies, Herr Kildedalen,' she said stiffly. 'In my—desire—to learn more about my aunt, I appear to have become sidetracked.'

The darkening of his expression told her that her apology had not gone down well. Indeed, he seemed more angered than ever. But he was to leave her shaken and momentarily stunned when, a second later, he let rip:

'Your sudden curiosity about your aunt is as false as the rest of you. Had you any real interest in her—any feeling for her at all—you'd have got up off your idle backside to come and see her when she wrote to say she was terminally ill.'

'I didn't know she was ill!' Zarah protested when she had her breath back. 'If she wrote, I never . . .'

'What a one you are for not receiving letters!' Stein jibed toughly.

'My aunt wrote—to me!'

'To your mother—it's the same thing.'

Even as Zarah told him, 'My mother never shared her letters with me,' a flash of memory darted in of a time when she had returned from shopping to see that her mother had been weeping. She had gone swiftly to her and had swallowed wholesale her mother's explanation that, in a weak moment, she had given way when the pain she had to endure had become too much. Only then did Zarah start to wonder. Her mother had been the bravest soul, and had never given way before. Had Anne's letter arrived, been read, and destroyed, while she had been out?

Suddenly she was aware of Stein Kildedalen silently watching her. 'I—didn't know, honestly I didn't,' she told him, and although there would have been many complications involved in leaving her mother for any length of time, she added, 'if my mother . . . my aunt . . . If I'd known more—I'd have got here somehow.'

'You broke all records getting here the moment you *did* know more,' Stein said cuttingly. 'Your feet didn't touch the ground when you heard you were likely to be a wealthy woman. You caught the very next ferry!'

Nettled, again Zarah wished he had been in the lawyer's office to hear that there had been a delay in writing to her. But since Stein was not going to believe her no matter how many times she told him she had not received Herr Langaard's letter, it was a shade sharply that she told him:

'When I left England, I didn't even know my aunt had died.'

He did not believe that either. He had her clean bowled, though, when, just as if he was giving her the benefit of the doubt—which she knew quite well he wasn't—he asked silkily:

'If you didn't know, if you were not—belatedly—journeying to Dalvik in response to Anne's letter telling you of her illness, why then, Miss Thornton, did you come?'

'I . . .' Feverishly she searched for some reason, other than the true reason. 'I came because . . .' Suddenly a heavensent reason dropped into her lap. But she saw she had hesitated for too long when, 'I came about—about the cottage,' she lied.

'Cottage?' he scoffed, and Zarah knew, even though no one could dispute the facts, that anything she added would be looked on by Stein as pure invention of the moment.

'The property my mother and I lived in was left jointly to my mother and her sister,' she told him nevertheless. 'A few weeks after my mother's death, I realised that I ought to come and see Aunt Anne to discuss what she wanted me to do about the property.' Not happy with lies, she had plodded on to a not so truthful end. But when Stein's expression showed nothing but blatant scepticism, all at once her temper overflowed. 'Oh, believe what you like!' she exploded suddenly. 'My coming to Dalvik has nothing to do with the fact that I might one day be a wealthy woman.' Angry, she saw no reason to let him know of the poor state of her present finances, and finally she slammed at him proudly, 'I wasn't exactly a pauper before my aunt named me in her will!'

Later, Zarah was to see that her last statement must have been like a red rag to a bull to Stein. For he was furious when, her explosion mild in comparison, he let go:

'You don't have to tell me that, you idle bitch! I've been paying your bills ever since I took the company over.'

'You've been paying ...!' Utterly astonished, Zara was nevertheless quick to recover. 'Don't be ridiculous,' she returned hotly. 'I ...'

'Ridiculous!' he chopped her off. 'I'll say it's ridiculous! While you were living a life of luxury, it was I who had to scrape along to make ends meet.' His fury rampant, as though in need of some action, he covered the space between them in a few strides and grabbed hold of her hands. 'Have these,' he thundered, the slender whiteness of her hands clearly offending him as he thrust them in front of her face, 'ever known a day's work?'

'I've never had a paid job, if that's what you're asking,' she replied, and strove hard not to be intimidated when his strong jaw jutted at a fierce angle and he threw her hands from him. 'My mother was an invalid and I was needed at home.' Her spirit started to revive, and suddenly she had started to hate him for making her confess to why she had not worked in paid employment. 'But there was no need for me to work anyway,' she went on in a flare of anger. 'The money from the trust fund my grandfather set up for my mother, *and* for my Aunt Anne,' she tossed in lest he thought his father had married into a family of down-and-outs, 'was more than adequate to keep us afloat.'

Argue that! she thought in triumph. To her disgust, Stein did not demean himself to argue, but, bestowing on her another of his superior looks, 'Anne was never in receipt of any money from England,' he told her bluntly.

'But she must have been! My grandfather was known for his fair-mindedness. He just wouldn't have made provision for one of his daughters and not the ...'

'The only money your aunt received,' Stein steamrollered in,' was money which came from Kildedalen Industrier. The same Kildedalen Industrier,' he added icily, 'which, while I toiled long into the night to make it a viable company, was constantly bled dry in order to give you a life of comfort.'

What he had just said would be appalling, and would more than account for the double-edged axe he had to grind with her—if it were true. But it was not true. Her mother had explained personally about that trust fund. Zarah remembered her mother, soft and warm-hearted, and knew that of the two, she could far more readily believe what her mother had told her than this granite-hard Norwegian who was as cold to her as his country's climate in winter.

Her bluntness was a match for his, ice in her voice too, when she did not back from telling him, 'Herr Kildedalen, I just don't believe you.'

To be called a liar had not endeared her to him, she quickly saw. 'You want proof?' he rapped, a muscle jerking in his temple. 'It's all there on record— confirmation of those quarterly additions to an already overburdened overdraft. Confirmation,' he gritted through his even white teeth, 'that whatever else was not paid, the first priority had to be a continuation of those payments to England.'

That Stein had referred to 'quarterly additions', when she had not told him the frequency of the payments from the trust fund, had the edge of doubt creeping in. Yet still she could not believe him.

'You're wrong,' she said. 'My mother told me . . .'

'What a lot you didn't share with her,' he sneered, in sarcastic reference to her telling him that her mother had never shared her mail with her. 'Naturally, you never once saw any notification either, that it was some idiot in Norway who was paying for your fancy clothes!'

For all the attention he had given her when, in her expensive dress, she had entered the dining-room, Zarah had thought that she, along with what she wore, had been

beneath his notice. But as doubt started to dig deeper and
it came to her that his sharp eyes missed not a thing, she
wished heartily that she had chosen to wear some chain-
store garment. She saw his eyes rest on her dress and
curvy form, and she was never more embarrassed in her
life. Doubt was suddenly rife, and even though she did
not want to believe it, the appalling revelations Stein had
made were starting to take shape as fact in her mind.

Aware that he was waiting for her to reply to his
sarcastic utterances, Zarah muttered, 'My mother was
trained in figure work. She was more than capable of—
handling our financial affairs without the need to call on
my untrained capabilities.'

'You certainly managed your financial affairs between
you better than I was able to handle mine in those early
days,' he grunted. And while, against what she wanted,
belief in all he had said started to set like concrete and
she began to feel sick inside, he appeared to reach boiling
point. And, as if the sight of her in his father's drawing
room was more than he could take, 'Why the hell don't
you go home?' he charged nastily.

At that moment, there was nothing Zarah would like
to have done better. She knew then that Stein hated her
as she hated him. But, when it was on the tip of her
tongue to tell him she would make straight for Bergen
and to a ferry to England in the morning—something
held her back. She knew immediately what that
something was. She still did not know which sister had
given her birth! Stein had had a good go at trampling her
pride in the dust, but even his loathing, his hatred of her,
was not sufficient, she realised, to have her turn her back
on her need to know.

Spirit, which was never very far from her, was
suddenly pushed to the fore. From somewhere too, Zara
dragged up what pride he had left her with, and her voice

was challenging, not timid, when in turn she charged:
'Why should I?'

She saw his eyes glint, and for a split second she was
fooled into thinking it was admiration that she refused to
be counted out. She knew that glint for the anger it was,
though, when with his customary hostility he replied:

'Leaving aside that it sticks in my gullet to have you
under this roof; you're a constant reminder to my father
of his dead wife.'

The fact that she was in search of every clue she could
glean enabled Zarah to ignore Stein Kildedalen's words
of unwelcome. She was impulsive again, when she asked
quickly, 'I look like Anne?'

Stein was good at attempting to freeze her with a look,
but Zarah refused to look away until, 'There's a family
likeness,' he told her coldly. 'You're quick, you're
intelligent, Miss Thornton, you must have noticed the
way my father kept looking at you during dinner.'

'I—did once,' she had to admit, 'but . . .' What she had
been going to add was lost when Stein cut in, to prick her
already badly bruised pride:

'Will you go back to England if I buy your shares from
you?'

Pride, and stubbornness, were suddenly on a side-by-
side march. She knew exactly why she would not return
to England—not yet anyway. But his insistence that she
should go, and go now, needled her. And, needled, he had
once more flushed out an insensitivity that was not
normally a part of her nature. Pride, stubbornness, were
joined by insensitivity, and she had no intention then of
giving way to that impulse that had come to her before he
had entered the drawing-room.

'Ah!' she retaliated, 'that's what is making you so mad,
isn't it? It's those shares, and the fact that I've got them,

and might—should there be another take-over bid—vote with the opposition.'

From the sudden jerking of his jaw, she saw that as he had needled her, so she had just needled him. 'You seem to have learned a great deal in a very short time,' he said grittily, and that needled her still more.

Somehow when Zarah sensed she might do better to cool what was becoming a worsening of a mutually aggressive atmosphere, something seemed to be compelling her to push him to the limits.

'What else did you expect?' she jeered. 'Surely, with your opinion of me so high,' she inserted sarcastically, 'you didn't think I'd pass up any opportunity to ferret out all I could?'

The clenching and unclenching of his hands at his sides told her that he found her sarcasm indigestible and that, if there was a chance he could get away with it, he could cheerfully throttle her. But, when she expected to receive a double helping of the sarcasm she had dished out, all he said after a few moments spent in deciding she was just not worth the sentence he would get for choking the life out of her was a curt:

'Well?'

Some devil was well and truly on her back. Or maybe it was her way of initially weathering the shock of realising that, all this time, her mother had lied to her about the source of their income. Either way, when Zarah quite well knew what Stein was asking, she pretended not to understand.

She gave an insolent shrug of her shoulders. 'Well—what?' she asked, careless that her attitude was goading.

'Damn you!' he thundered. 'Will you return to England?'

The grim look of his jaw warned her that she might yet feel the pressure of his hands around her throat—but, whatever it was in charge of her, it still refused to let her back down.

'Oh, you'd just love that, wouldn't you?' she jibed. 'You can't wait for an opportunity to tell Herr Langaard that I've broken the terms of my aunt's will and have left Norway in under six months!' The sudden blaze of fury in his eyes told her she had gone too far. But, pushed on, by what she knew not, Zarah went further, and finally succeeded in pushing Stein over the limits. 'That way,' she threw at him insultingly, 'you wouldn't have to pay me at all!'

The words were barely off her tongue when, outraged, Stein grabbed a savage hold of her. 'First you call me a liar,' he snarled through gritted teeth, his grip biting into her upper arms, 'and now you call me a cheat. My God,' he roared, enraged, 'do you ask for it!'

Panic, when his hands snaked from her arms to her throat, caused her to move quickly, her quick movement throwing her off balance. But even as she fell against him she managed to bring her arms up and between his to break his hold.

Her relief was shortlived when his hands came away from her throat. But as he took his hands away from her, Zarah found that she was held in his arms.

Frantically she tried to struggle out of his hold but, infuriated by her, Stein refused to let her go. Her eyes met his in silent combat, but at the gleam that came to his grey eyes as she fought to be free, Zarah knew that he was under no illusions of how loathsome she found his touch.

When his head started to come down to meet hers, she knew what that gleam in his eyes was all about. Stein, aware of her hate, had just thought of a way to punish her which excluded the possibility of him landing up on a murder charge.

She felt his mouth on hers, and fought him furiously.

He broke his kiss. 'Let me go, you . . .' His mouth again over hers silenced her. She felt the pressure of his arms around her increase, and as he hauled her closer to him, suddenly there was not a glimmer of light between them. His mouth was harsh and cruel on hers and, as he meant it to be, punishing.

Why then did she suddenly feel a strange tingling all over her body? Her body could not escape the close contact with his hard-muscled body, but, when her brain urgently instructed her to fight on, all at once she experienced a stronger impulse not to comply.

Then, as her fists ceased to pummel his shoulders and flattened out into hands that simply held on to him because she seemed incapable of doing anything else, the hard bruising pressure of his lips gentled out. Suddenly, though he still held her tight, Stein's mouth was no longer punishing. Suddenly, his mouth was gentle, his lips inviting hers apart. Suddenly, he was expertly searching for a response. And, just as suddenly, Zarah found—she was responding.

Which one of them came to their senses first, she was too confused to know. But as Stein moulded her to him, and she melted against him, an awareness of what she was doing finally hit her full square. And at that exact moment of her pulling back, Stein thrust her from him.

Shaken though she was that she could have responded so to a man she hated, one look at his soon adopted hostile expression told Zarah that something guaranteed to be insulting was on its way.

'My word, Stein,' she got in first, giving herself a mental kick that his first name had slipped out, 'you really are desperate for those shares, aren't you?' Hastily, when it looked as though a murder trial might have some attractions for him after all, she backed away. She was over by the door, Stein at a safe distance away, when, sweetly, she dared, 'Sorry I can't oblige. But, with those shares going up in value all the time, I'd be an idiot to sell just now—don't you think?' She did not wait for his answer, but, as he started to move, she fled. Zarah did not sleep well that night. There was too much going on in her head for sleep to have much of a chance. She did not want to think about the way Stein had kissed her, or about the way she had responded when his kisses had become not punishing but—pleasurable. Instead, she went over the conversation she'd had with him in the drawing-room. The word 'conversation', in her view, was a polite term for the verbal warfare that had gone on.

Away from him and his dominant character, though, she suddenly found it too incredible to believe that her mother had lied to her about that trust fund. Stein, on the other hand, with his aversion to being called a liar, had been adamant that their quarterly income came from him. He had even suggested he could show her proof of those quarterly payments. Not that she would lower herself to ask to see anything of the kind.

In search of the truth, Zarah nagged at the subject, but her search was barren and an hour later she could see only one solution. She could not wait for a reply to any letter she wrote to the bank, so on Monday she would telephone England.

Strangely, when to speak with the bank manager had become important and urgent, her last waking thought was not of the telephone call she would make. Stein, his mouth gentle over hers, was the last thing she remembered when sleep eventually claimed her.

CHAPTER FIVE

By Monday, Zarah was more familiar with the layout of Haldor Kildedalen's home. It took her longer to recover from her call to the bank manager in England.

She had been uncertain whether he would discuss her dead mother's business affairs over the telephone. But she need not have worried. That she was ringing from Norway seemed enough to bear out the authenticity of her saying who she was.

'Where better to be at this time of your sad loss than with other members of your family?' he had said sympathetically.

Her surprise that he knew she had kinfolk in Norway almost made her blurt out as much. By some miracle, she checked, and was able to see it as perfectly feasible that her mother might have told the bank manager at some time or other that she had a sister in Norway.

'I came to my relatives on the spur of the moment.' she told him, and went into her planned routine. 'I'm afraid—with leaving in such a hurry—that I've over-looked one or two matters which I really should have dealt with before I left England.'

'That's quite understandable,' he answered kindly, then asked, 'How can I help? Are you short of funds?' he queried.

Zarah put a smile into her voice to tell him, 'Oh no, it's nothing like that.' He would soon enough discover the poor state of her finances. 'It's just that, while I assumed my mother's bank account would be frozen until her estate is settled, it has only just occurred to me—with so many other people to notify,' she dropped in, 'that I've not notified anyone *officially* that the quarterly deposits of money into her account should be cancelled.' In some confusion as she came to an end, Zarah had the feeling she had come unstuck when, with a degree of puzzlement in his voice, the bank manager asked:

'You wish me to write an official notification for you, Miss Thornton?'

She had to go on. 'No, I can do that,' she said quickly. 'But I don't have the address with me.' She was then almost floored when, hearing rustling sounds suggesting he was consulting papers which must have been brought to him as her call was put through, she heard him ask:

'Er—Herr Stein Kildedalen—he *does* know of your mother's death?'

Zarah gripped hard onto the phone and fought for control to tell him, 'Of course. B—but since it was my mother herself who taught me that business matters should be kept strictly as business matters, I really feel she would want me to put into writing . . .'

'Quite so, quite so,' he agreed quickly and proceeded to dictate an address which she did not bother to take down. With or without an official notification, Stein Kildedalen would not be sending so much as another penny to England, she was sure of that.

Zarah came away from the phone in a state of near collapse. When her brain did begin to function again, she was on a fresh treadmill of asking—why?

It was as clear as day: Aunt Anne must have been the instigator behind those quarterly payments—but why? Supposing her sister had been having a hard time to bring up a child without an income—would Anne ask Haldor to make her an allowance? Even if it was to the financial detriment of his firm? Zarah's stomach knotted up when back came the answer—she might, for love of her own child.

The next question to hit Zarah was, would Haldor agree to Anne's request without first knowing some more concrete reason to cripple his firm than that her sister was in something of a financial hole?

Zarah wanted desperately to ask Haldor Kildedalen what he knew. But memory was quick to remind her that that deeply depressed man was the last person she could ask. Stein too was out.

With Stein in her head, she had to take a moment to oust the recurring memory of his mouth gentle on hers. But she just had to query—why had Stein kept up those quarterly payments when he had taken over the business?

Why should he? Olav Langaard had told her of the struggle it had been for Stein to keep the company in existence, so why had Stein allowed the firm's precious resources to be siphoned off? Why, when he had taken over, had he not cancelled those payments but continued to make them? Without question he would have asked his father about those quarterly amounts which had pushed the firm further into the red. But if Haldor knew anything significant, he could not have told him or, blunt as usual, Stein would have referred to it.

It did not take Zarah long to see why, when it was in Stein's power to stop those payments, he had not done so. It all came down to his love and respect for his father. For him to keep a couple of Englishwomen in comfort and yet remain in the dark as to why he should do so endorsed for her what she had seen with her own eyes, that Stein had a genuine love and respect for his parent.

By Wednesday she had been forced to accept that every word Stein had said was the truth. It had been hard to swallow that, compared to the way he had scraped along, his hard work had kept her in a clover-like existence. She blanched each time she thought of how his night-and-day labour had paid for her upkeep and the very clothes she was wearing. As a result, she was grateful not to have to see him too often.

The reason why she so seldom saw him stemmed from his caring for his father. Haldor's concentration, it seemed, had suffered to such an extent since he had lost his wife that, for the time being, he had given up driving. Stein, in his endeavours to get his father out of the house for some part of each day, would take him off on some outing or other.

Restless still to know the truth of whose child she was, Zarah was in her room with a few minutes to go before she went down to dinner, when she suddenly started to wonder—what was the point in prolonging her stay in Norway? Aside from learning that there had never been any trust fund, and having to accept that everything she stood up in had been paid for by Stein, she had learned nothing more.

With his father still deeply depressed, she had ceased to hope that Haldor might perhaps let slip some small piece of information to add weight to her suspicion that Anne, and not her sister Margaret, had been her mother. Indeed, so unhappy was he that even his interest in a boat he owned had gone. The boat, she had gleaned, had been a source of much pleasure to him and Anne. But only that morning, when Stein had suggested at breakfast that they go and check the boat over, his father had wearily replied that he intended to sell it.

Dinner followed the same pattern of every other meal, with Haldor eating little, and not saying very much. By then Zarah was used to the way she would occasionally look up and find that his eyes were on her.

It happened again as she popped a morsel of fish into

her mouth. She glanced across the table and caught him looking at her. She smiled, because there was little else she could do, but as she turned her head slightly, she caught Stein looking at them both.

Somehow, when Stein switched his glance wholly on to her, she managed to hang on to her smile. But as she read in his cold look a reiteration of his 'Why the hell don't you go home?' she could not help but feel nettled.

'This sole,' she said pleasantly, returning her attention to her fish, 'is absolutely delicious.' She had addressed no one in particular, but it was Stein who replied.

'You'll have to take what comes tomorrow.' As ever in front of his father, his tone was civil. 'Fru Onsvag has Thursdays off.'

Zarah debated whether to make some equally 'civil'-sounding rejoinder when, albeit half to himself, Haldor Kildedalen suddenly spoke. 'Anne always insisted on taking over on Fru Onsvag's day off,' he stated. And while from Stein's sudden stillness Zarah received the impression that this was the first time he had heard Anne's name on his father's lips since she had died, his father continued, 'Anne used to say that Thursdays were her only chance to play at being a housewife.'

The room seemed strangely hushed when he finished speaking, and as she experienced a rush of feeling for her aunt's husband, Zarah wondered if he had just taken the first step in coming to terms with his grief.

He had started to retreat into his grief-ridden shell when the impulsive part of her nature would not be denied. 'Uncle Haldor,' she gently attracted his attention, 'would you—be offended,' she asked tentatively, 'if I tried my hand in the kitchen tomorrow?'

Long moments passed before he answered, and she feared she might have intruded too far. She rode Stein's hostile look. But when previously he would have butted

in, for once he held back on his protection towards his
father, and waited, as she did, for him to make his own
reply.

'This is your home now, Zarah,' he answered as last.
'Please feel free to do as you wish.'

She thought it hardly an enthusiastic invitation for her
to take over the kitchen, but his saying it was her home
now made her send him a warm, 'Thank you.'

It was not of Haldor Kildedalen she was thinking
when she lay down in her bed a few hours later, however,
but his son. She had ignored the look Stein had thrown
her, but it had registered just the same. Quite clearly, it
was his opinion that he would be eating some burnt
offering if tomorrow saw her let loose amongst the
housekeeper's pots and pans.

Breakfast was no problem when she raided the larder
the following morning. Haldor was content with a lightly
boiled egg and some thinly sliced bread and butter. Stein,
she left to help himself from the basket of bread which
she placed alongside a cheese plate and a selection of cold
meats. She sat down with them, but as soon as she had
finished her bowl of cereal, she took herself back to the
kitchen.

She had observed that the kitchen window looked out
on to a lawn bordered by flower beds. In the act of
restoring packets and packages to their cupboards, she
paused to take a longer look. Marigolds and marguerites
splashed orange and white to blend with pastel-shaded
snapdragons. In the centre of the lawn, red, yellow and
pink roses nodded good morning to multi-coloured asters
and orange lilies. The effect, Zarah saw, was that of an
English country garden. She was certain then that her
aunt had created this garden, and that she had loved it.

Zarah dwelt for some minutes on the quiet and restful
scene, until the fluttering of a white butterfly as it settled

on a rose distracted her attention. She resumed her chores, but in the middle of washing the breakfast dishes, she was again attracted to the window. Haldor Kildedalen had come into the garden. He, like his son, was tall. But where Stein was upright and walked with a purposeful stride, Haldor, weighed down with his sorrow, was stooped over and his gait uncertain.

He was much too taken up with his private thoughts to ever notice her watching him, but all the same, to do so seemed an intrusion into his privacy. Zarah looked away and involved herself with the washing up once more. But when a feeling of affection for him, which had grown without her knowing it, had her wanting to check that he was all right, she again looked out.

He was still there. Only now he was bent over and was snipping off a posy. She had no need to be told, she just knew, that the simple marigolds and daisies had been her aunt's favourite flowers. Just as she knew that Haldor was cutting the flowers to take to the cemetery.

His task completed, she watched him leave the garden. Sorely then did she feel a desire to go with him. Whether her Aunt Anne had been just her aunt, or as paper evidence said, her mother, she felt overcome by a need to want to go to the graveside to pay her respects. Again, a fear of intruding on Haldor Kildedalen's privacy held her back.

Zarah was tidying the kitchen when she heard Stein's car being started up and driven off. Whether he had taken his father out for the day or whether they would be back at lunch time, she did not know. What she did know, however, was that their first stop would be the cemetery.

The kitchen was as immaculate as she had found it when, in a solemn frame of mind, Zarah wondered what she should do next. Her newly discovered affection for the man who had asked her to call him 'Uncle' gave her the answer.

Armed with a duster, she was soon at work in his sitting room making it more comfortable for him to come home to. The cushions in his favourite chair plumped up and inviting, she dusted round until she came to a small bureau to the left of one wall. Absorbed as she was in what she was doing, it never crossed her mind that the bureau could well be locked when, intent not to leave a dust line at the pull-down flap, she pulled back the flap—and paused.

Suddenly she remembered Stein saying she had a family likeness to her aunt. But she had never ever seen a photograph of her. Yet, if there was a picture of Anne anywhere, surely it would be in this room that Haldor favoured more than any other. Had it been more than he could take to have her picture there and not his dear Anne in person? Had he put her picture away—in this very bureau—until such time as he felt able to take it out again?

Without conscious thought, guided only by a compulsion to see how much like her aunt she was, Zarah pulled the flap all the way down. With urgent fingers, she began to investigate the inside of the bureau. But she did not get very far, for suddenly an infuriated bellow rent the air.

'How—*dare*—you?'

On a gasp, Zarah whirled round to see that while she had been oblivious to anything but her compulsion to find a photograph of her aunt, Stein, an outraged Stein, had returned home to find her rifling through his father's papers.

'I—c-can explain,' she spluttered, fear and alarm seizing her when, furious, Stein moved towards her.

Her guilty expression, she gathered swiftly, meant he did not intend to listen to a word of her explanation.

Without regard that her fingers might well have been caught in the flap, he slammed the bureau flap hard shut. The next thing she knew, he had grabbed her none too ceremoniously by one wrist and was hauling her after him from the room.

Made to run to keep up with him, that or measure her length, Zarah was still trying to convince him, 'It's—not—what—you—think,' when, incensed, he dragged her into a room which she knew to be a study.

His distaste evident, he threw her burning wrist from him and went to hoist several box files from off the top of a cabinet. Zarah was still trying to get her breath back when he stabbed a finger in the direction of a wall safe that had been hidden by the files.

'To save you lifting the floorboards,' he grated bitingly, 'anything of value is kept in there.'

'I wasn't . . .'

'*My God!*' he thundered over the top of anything she would have protested. 'To think you, my father's guest . . .' His look murderous, his rage went into overdrive. 'Open it!' he roared. 'The combination is your aunt's birthdate. Since your avarice would have you steal from her husband, *open it*!'

At that, her pride in an uproar to be so accused, Zarah's own fury awoke. 'I wasn't trying to steal,' she erupted angrily.

'I saw you.' he slammed back. 'You . . .'

'You saw me looking for a photograph of my aunt.' She was too incensed herself by then to think of hiding the truth. 'You said there was a family likeness,' she sprinted on. 'I've never seen a picture of her, so I just . . .'

'Wanted to satisfy your curiosity?' he cut her off, and let her know what he thought of her explanation when he barked, 'You're the end! All these years you've been content to sit back and take and take, without once writing to ask for a picture of her! All these years, when you knew that but for her you would be without an income, you showed no curiosity. Yet now, I'm to believe your curiosity became too much for you?'

By the time he had finished, Zarah's anger had quieted sufficiently for her to realise she could not tell him the reason for her sudden curiosity. In contrast, though, her excuse seemed to have angered him the more, and she backed in fear when, his jaw jutting at an aggressive angle, he caught hold of her still burning wrist a second time.

She had no idea where he was taking her when he pulled her after him out of the study, but when at the bottom of the stairs he turned to go up, it was not mere fear that gripped her, but terror. She had seen him furious before, and had never forgotten that, when his fury had needed an outlet that time, he had kissed her. To her terror-stricken eyes his fury now seemed greater than it had been then. And suddenly, as he prised her glued-fast fingers off the banister and half carried her up the stairs, the word 'Rape!' screamed in her head.

'Let me go!' she screeched as Stein pushed her into a large bedroom and the unmade double bed took her alarm into giant proportions.

'With the greatest of pleasure,' he retorted, and suddenly she was free.

'W-what—are you—going to do?' she panted, her eyes fastened on him as she backed away.

She saw surprise take him as he caught her drift, but she felt neither insulted nor offended, only relieved, when sarcastically, he scorned, 'God help me I should ever be so hard up!'

Her fear started to depart when, as he strode to the bedside table, she spotted a pair of slippers which she had last seen adorning his father's feet. Surely he would never commit such an act of violation in his father's bedroom?

All the same, she eyed Stein warily when he took up a framed photograph and thrust it into her hands. Then fury, fear and any other agitated emotion in her promptly died.

The photograph was of Anne. It had to be. Zarah was barely aware of Stein as she studied the portrait of a still lovely smiling woman of about forty. There was a clear family resemblance in the same brown eyes, the same dark hair, the same dainty but straight nose. The same chin too, she saw. But, and to bring the sting of tears to her eyes, what struck Zarah most was not that she resembled her aunt, but that her aunt looked so very much like a younger version of her mother.

Love for her dead mother welled up, and suddenly Zarah knew, if she was not to break down in front of Stein, that she was going to have to stop looking at the photograph.

Brushing past him, she returned the picture to the bedside table, and would have slipped from the room without comment. Would have, if Stein had not caught hold of her arm and swung her around to face him.

She did not want to raise her head, but a firm hand under her chin propelled her head upward. 'Tears?' he grunted sceptically, when, forcing her to look at him, he spotted the shine in her eyes.

Her emotions were too much out of gear for her to find anything at all snappy with which to reply to his scepticism. She was still striving for control, when the husky words slipped out, 'Anne—m-my aunt—she reminded me of my mother.'

For long seconds Stein stared into her liquid brown eyes. Then all at once, his harsh expression had changed. She felt his grip on her arm ease to a more gentle hold.

Gentle too was his voice, the scepticism gone when with
a never-before-known sympathy, he said quietly:

'You lost her only a short time ago.'

Bemused to hear his sympathy, Zarah could only stare.
Surprise kept her dumb. But that surprise was the start of
her getting back on to a more even keel. She was jerked
all the way back to a more real world when with his grey
eyes scrutinising her face, Stein suddenly murmured:

'Beauty, Zarah, appears to run in your family.'

To hear a compliment from his lips, when up until then
all she had heard from him was the exact opposite,
caused Zarah to wake up suddenly. Stein hated her, she
knew he did. Her near-tears must have triggered off a
kinder side of his nature, but it would not last. He would
be doubly insulting to her then because he had let her
near-tears get to him, she just knew it. She recalled all the
unpleasant things he had said to her—how, only a short
while ago he had been ready to brand her as a thief.

The snappiness she had wanted before was then there
in an abundant supply. 'Watch it, Kildedalen!' she
snorted waspishly, and wrenched free of his loose hold.
She ignored the instant hostility in his expression—she
was more familiar with his dark looks anyway. 'Next
thing you know, you'll be apologising for accusing me of
having sticky fingers!'

That did it. She did not have to say more. Zarah saw
from the glint in his eye just before he strode to the door
that reminding him of how he had caught her with her
fingers inside his father's bureau had just ensured he
would never be so forgetful again. His granite-hard
expression underlined the fact that should she weep non-
stop for the rest of her stay, he would never again show
her an atom of sympathy.

When he showed no intention of going further than the
door until she had left his father's room, Zarah moved

forward. Then, suddenly, she halted.

'Where's your father?' she asked.

A world of arrogance broke through the cold mask of Stein's expression, and she thought she was going to be damned for an answer. But, his impatience showing, she gathered it was that impatience to have her out of his sight which made him reply curtly:

'He wanted a half-hour on his own.'

From that Zarah gleaned that, respecting his father's wish to be alone at Anne's graveside, Stein had dropped him off at the cemetery, and had returned home to while away the time until he went back for him.

She took another step towards the door, but as she did, she caught sight of the unmade bed. There was no way then that she could leave the poor man's bed like that. In a trice she was stripping it, glancing at Stein only when she heard his impatient movement.

'I presume,' she said tartly, intent on ignoring how he appeared to be doing the Norwegian equivalent of counting up to ten, 'that you're big enough to make your own.'

'You keep out of my room,' he threatened ominously.

'I should ever be so hard up!' she bounced back insolently—then found, when it had never been in her mind to ask such a question that she was asking, 'Why— whose picture do you have by your bedside?'

'No conniving raven-haired Englishwoman, you can be sure of that!' he grated. The slam of the bedroom door told her that anything else she had to say could be said to herself.

In less than a minute, Zarah was wondering—why on earth had she asked him whose picture did he have at his bedside? For goodness' sake, she wasn't in the least interested!

Strangely, though, she experienced the most peculiar

feeling at the thought of some unconniving, blonde-haired Norwegian girl sharing his room with him.

She finished making the bed, but with the room generally tidy, there was nothing more she could do for Haldor's comfort. She went to the photograph of her aunt, and felt stronger than she had before when she saw how like her mother her aunt had been. Zarah recalled the unexpected sympathy she had seen in Stein when he had seen the shine of tears in her eyes, and suddenly she felt an almost overwhelming feeling of regret. Stein had reacted to her small show of grief as any man might, and she—she had rejected his sympathy in no uncertain fashion.

The thought—could her regret stem from a need to want Stein to stay kind and gentle to her?—made Zarah hasten from the room. Good lord, what was she thinking of? She made her way to the kitchen, and by the time she got there had assured herself that, being used by now to Stein being a pig to her, she didn't give a button.

It was a beautiful summer's day. She made a salad for lunch, and ate it at her usual place at the table. When Haldor was looking, she smiled and passed the odd comment to Stein here and there. When he was not looking, she ignored his son, and Stein, anxious that his father should not be disturbed any more than he was, acted likewise. But, batting away his killing look on one occasion, Zarah was in no doubt that she needn't look at him for mouth-to-mouth resuscitation should his look have killed.

After lunch she washed up, then looked to see what there was for dinner. The freezer revealed multitudinous fare. Chicken, she considered, would take too long to thaw out, and while the idea of giving Stein a generous helping of salmonella had definite appeal, there was his father to consider. She opted for steak with a red wine sauce, with a pear shortcake to follow.

The menu decided upon, but with some hours to go before she needed to make a start, Zarah took herself off for a walk. Restless, she wondered again if she would never know peace.

She took an opposite route from the way she usually went. With no specific destination in mind, she kept to a road that ran alongside the fjord when suddenly she realised that since her other walks had shown no sign of a cemetery, that perhaps the cemetery lay this way.

Stein had opted to return home to wait the half-hour his father had needed alone, so surely the journey between the house and the cemetery could not take many minutes? If it was too far distant, Stein would have waited for him nearby, wouldn't he?

Endeavouring not to be distracted by the magnificent view, Zarah walked on, not ready, now she had some aim in mind, to give up easily. But she had gone a fair way when she had to accept that the cemetery must lie in the opposite direction after all.

She halted, to pause and look around. Then as she noticed where the road curved round a mountain, it seemed to her that since she had come all this way, she might as well carry on that bit further. It could quite well be that what she was seeking lay just around the corner.

The road around the corner dipped back from the water. In an inlet that held a small line of hire craft, Zarah saw a man bent over in the act of repairing one of them.

As she was about to go by, the man looked up and saw her. *'God dag,'* he called, and straightened away from his work.

'God dag,' she returned, then saw that even those two small words had given away that her accent was not Norwegian.

'You are American?' he queried, and without more ado he came over to her.

He was a man of average height, in his late twenties, good-looking, and to Zarah's mind, aware of the fact. But, given he had a flirtatious look in his eye, he appeared quite harmless.

'I'm English,' she said, and took the opportunity to ask, 'Can you tell me where the cemetery is?'

'Cemetery!' For a moment she wondered if it was a word he did not understand. He had asked her if she was American in quite good English, though.

'My aunt, Fru Kildedalen —— ' she started to explain, but had no need to continue.

'Ah! You wish to see where she—rests,' he comprehended, and before she knew it he had taken hold of her right hand, shaken it, and was introducing himself. 'My name is Rolv Fjeld,' he said, flashing her a white-toothed smile.

'Zarah Thornton,' she murmured, and retrieved her hand.

'You are staying in Dalvik?'

Zarah nodded. 'With —my uncle, Herr Kildedalen.'

'A sad time,' he commiserated. 'A very sad time. I have seen Herr Kildedalen not knowing where he is in his loss. He and your aunt had much closeness.'

'They were devoted,' she said quietly, and would have again asked directions, only Rolv Fjeld took up:

'It is said his love for his wife was a possessive love.' Slightly shaken to hear such a statement, Zarah was none the less of the view that she did not want to speak to this man of something that was so personal to her host. But before she could say a cool good afternoon and go on her way, Rolv Fjeld had gone on to say something which had her feet glued to the concrete. 'It was so from the beginning,' he said. 'My mother often mentioned the time when Fru Kildedalen first came to Norway. She and a friend called at the little house to show friendship, but when Fru Kildedalen—she was not Fru Kildedalen then,' he put in with another flash of his teeth, 'but when she offered them tea, Herr Kildedalen sat with them, because, my mother says, he could not bear to have his future bride from him for very long.'

All the time he was talking, Zarah was wondering about her own lack of brain power. Aunt Anne had lived in Norway for twenty-one years, for goodness' sake, and must have made many friends. Why hadn't she thought of that? Surely one of those friends would know by what name she had been known by before she had married Haldor?

'I expect my aunt had many friends in the village?' she asked, impatient to learn all she could.

'Fru Kildedalen was friendly with everyone,' she was informed. 'But she went nowhere without her husband, I think.'

'Oh,' said Zarah, and hid her disappointment under a mumbled, 'I thought, since she lived here for such a long time . . .'

'She didn't live in Dalvik originally,' he told her. 'I think Herr Kildedalen rented a small holiday home that first summer she came. But she must have loved Dalvik very much, because when Kildedalen Industrier began to prosper, he had the much larger home he has now built, ready for his retirement.'

The talkative Norwegian went on to explain that the retirement age in Norway was officially sixty-seven, according to one's occupation, but how Herr Kildedalen had retired earlier than that to be with his wife all the time. But save for Zarah realising that Haldor must be nearer to sixty-five than the seventy-five which, on account of his grief, he looked, she learned nothing of what she was after. Though when Rolv Fjeld finally ran out of words, she doggedly made another attempt.

'So it was when my aunt came here that first summer that your mother made friends with her?'

'As much as she could,' Rolv said with another grin. 'But a lot has happened since then. My parents are now divorced and married to other people. My mother,' he told her cheerfully, 'is now living in America.'

Tenacity had got her nowhere. Ready to wish the boat repairer goodbye, Zarah then realised that she had not hidden her disappointment as well as she had thought.

'I have upset you in some way?' asked Rolv, donning such an air of being ready to cut out his tongue that, womaniser though he obviously was, she felt obliged to tell him:

'No, of course not.' He did not look convinced. 'I'm not at all upset,' she stayed to endorse. 'It's just that—I didn't know my aunt very well, and I feel I should like to have done.' Tenacity was at her elbow again when she tried one last feeler. 'I feel, if I could have spoken with someone who knew her before she changed her name to Kildedalen, that I would have a base from which to start knowing more.'

His expression was full of regret when he told her he could not help her there. 'Everyone locally has only known her as Fru Kildedalen,' he said positively.

Zarah forced a smile, after which there was nothing more to be said but to ask for directions to the cemetery a second time. She learned that the cemetery was but a short walk away, and having bidden him goodbye, she left him.

She found her aunt's grave without any trouble. As yet there was no headstone, but the marigolds and marguerites which she had seen Haldor select from the garden stood out from the floral tributes on the other graves.

A semblance of peace came over her as she gave up a prayer for her aunt. But that peace was brief. Before she turned from the graveside, there again to nag her was the question, 'Who are you, Anne—aunt or mother?'

She had no wish to get into conversation with Rolv Fjeld when she passed him on her return, so she kept up a smart pace. 'Thank you,' she waved a hand to indicate that his directions had been accurate, and went smartly on.

It was a long walk back, and she approached the house knowing that she had been out for some good while. She, it appeared, was not the only one aware of the length of her absence. For no sooner had she got the front door open than Stein appeared in the hall to demand:

'Where have you been?'

Zarah's first reaction was to wonder if something dreadful had happened to Haldor, but she cancelled that reaction. If anything had happened to his father, Stein would have handled it without requiring her help.

'If it's any concern of yours,' she sarcastically followed through with her second reaction, 'I've been to the cemetery.'

She had rather hoped that would stump him for a reply, but it didn't. 'How did you get there?' he asked tersely.

'I walked,' she snapped. 'There and back,' and to show him how it was done, she walked straight past him to the kitchen.

Her labours in the kitchen paid off in that everything turned out the way it was meant to. Haldor, although his appetite had not improved, seemed to enjoy what he had eaten. 'Thank you, Zarah,' he said when the meal was over, 'that was good.'

She smiled at him, and got up to clear the used dishes away. 'Thank you, Zarah,' said Stein when she neared him, and lowered his voice to add, 'that was—passable.'

Though she was certain that, had Haldor not been there, she would have cracked the plate in her hand over Stein's head, all she could do, since he was there, was to hiss, 'Don't fall over yourself!' The next moment she felt an utter fool—because that was just what she almost did. For as she turned hotly away from Stein, her foot went under, and she very nearly fell over her own feet.

She limped a step or two until she had got her full balance, but was then astonished to hear Haldor, his voice holding a sharp note for the first time, ask, 'You still suffer with your walking, Zarah?'

It took a second or two for her to realise what he must be talking about. Then, taken totally aback, 'You know about my hospital treatment?' she questioned.

'You were in hospital when Anne left England,' he replied. 'Naturally your mother wrote to tell us of your surgery.' He drifted off for a few seconds and Zarah, startled still, thought that was all he was going to say on the subject. But he added quietly, 'I seem to recall a later letter where Margaret said you would sometimes limp when you were overtired.'

'I'm fine now,' she assured him, her heart starting to bump as she wondered if she dared probe to find out what else had been written between the two sisters.

She racked her brains for words in which she might sensitively, tactfully learn if Anne and her mother had been closer than she had always thought. So close, in fact, that they would have done anything for each other. But Zarah had delayed too long, and she could have hit Stein when he turned the conversation away from where she wanted it, to butt in suddenly:

'You have a fear of flying—were you in the same aircrash that killed your father?'

'No,' she said shortly, thanking him neither for his

reminder of her idiotic phobia nor for his interruption.

'But you do have a disability?'

Zarah almost flared a snappy answer, but in time she remembered Haldor. 'I have no disability whatsoever,' she replied as coolly as she dared with his father present. A flicked glance at Stein showed he wanted more.

Thinking he could take a running jump, she saw that determined something in his expression which said that if she didn't tell him all there was to tell, he would ask and ask until he did know it all. Which, if she was to hang on to her outward show of civility, with his father present she was going to have to answer anyway.

'I was born prematurely,' she resigned herself to reveal. 'It was thought I would never walk, but when I was two, I had an operation which cleared the defect.'

'You were in hospital until you were two years old?'

'I remember nothing of it,' she replied shortly. 'And there's absolutely nothing wrong with me now.' Already agitated that her chance to find out more from Haldor was getting away from her, Zarah wanted to gag Stein, when he persisted:

'But you still have to guard against becoming overtired?'

'No,' she muttered between her teeth. 'The limp my mother referred to must have been in my growing years when perhaps I'd played too vigorous a game of tennis or netball.'

She glanced at Haldor, to see that he had once more withdrawn himself—her opportunity to try and probe deeper probably gone for ever. Anger against Stein stewed inside her as she loaded more dishes on to a tray. Then she found, as she went to take the tray from the room, that Stein was there trying to take the tray from her.

'I'll attend to these,' he said firmly when she refused to let go her hold.

'Oh, for goodness' sake!' she exploded, forgetful, as her anger with him broke out, that his father was there.

'I've said I'll clear away and do the washing up,' Stein insisted toughly, every bit as stubborn as she.

Angrily, Zarah refused to yield. She wished she had never told him that she had walked the long distance to and from the cemetery. Sweetly, though, to intrude on her irritation at being treated like some invalid, she remembered the pots and pans, as high as Norway's Jotunheim mountains, all waiting to be washed.

'Don't complain to me if you get dishpan hands,' she said shortly, and pushed the tray at him.

She would then have stormed, limp-free, from the room. Only just in time did she remember that she had not said good night to his father. Only then, in fact, did she remember that Haldor Kildedalen was in the same room—as her and Stein!

Quickly she glanced at Haldor, concerned that he might be upset at the way she and his son had been ready to go for each other. Her surprises for the day were not over.

Always before, she and Stein had been studiously polite in his company, and never once had she seen Haldor smile. Yet, incredibly, to have just seen her and his son strike sparks off each other had brought a smile to Haldor's face!

CHAPTER SIX

ZARAH finished what had now become her daily
constitutional in sombre mood. She had met no one who
had known her aunt before she had changed her name to
Kildedalen. It was only an outside chance anyway, but
ever since she had come across Rolv Fjeld a week ago
yesterday, she had lived in hope of maybe meeting
someone who had known her aunt in those early days.

Zarah walked up the drive to the house, wondering at
the stubbornness that kept her in Norway, for it seemed
she was no further forward than she had ever been.

Haldor, whose first smile had been his one and only,
was mostly in a world of his own and would not miss her
if she was not there. As for Stein, he couldn't wait to see
the back of her.

She shrugged away the thought that to inherit those
shares meant that she had to stay in Norway for six
months. She had not got around to deciding what she was
going to do about those shares. Haldor had given them to
Anne out of his deep love for her—was it not only right
that the shares should be returned to him?

Zarah entered the house and could not, in any case, see
herself staying under the same roof as Stein Kildedalen
for the remaining months. And since her funds wouldn't
run to her putting up at even the most inexpensive
pensjonat for that length of time, to return to England
seemed to be the only answer.

She was halfway up the stairs when a door opened and
she heard the sound of Stein's tread. She was near the top
of the stairs when she heard him call curtly:

'Telephone!'

Since she was the only one he reserved that tone of voice for, Zarah turned round. 'For me?' Stein did not bother to reply, but swung away and went from her view.

Curiosity sent her after him. Apart from the bank manager, no other person in England knew she was in Norway. She reached the bottom of the stairs and decided that the call could not be from England. Though since she knew no one else, it could quite possibly be the lawyer, Olav Langaard. Why he should be telephoning, however, she could not fathom.

The only door open in the hall was the study door. Zarah went in, to see that Stein was sitting behind a huge desk, and had resumed whatever he had been doing before the phone rang. She knew, when he did not so much as look up, that she would be wasting her time asking him to leave so she could take her call in private. Though since he had probably grilled the lawyer pretty thoroughly about her inheritance, she rather supposed there was nothing Herr Langaard had to discuss which he did not know about.

She presented Stein with her back as she picked up the phone and said, 'Hello.' It was not Olav Langaard at the other end.

'Rolv Fjeld here. I am happy you are still in Dalvik,' said the man she had met once and had forgotten all about. 'I was not certain that your holiday might be over and that you had gone to England.'

'I'm . . .' still here, she had been going to say, simply because she could not think of anything else to say. But an imp of mischief suddenly entered her soul and, in the sincere hope that Stein was listening—and she couldn't see how he could avoid hearing her side of the conversation, 'Norway is such a beautiful country,' she told Rolv, 'that I've no intention of leaving in a hurry.'

'That pleases me very much,' he replied warmly. 'I wish to ask you to have dinner with me tonight.'

Zarah knew it was the moment to back off. He was a pleasant enough man, but he fancied himself as a lady-killer, and the flirty gleam she remembered in his eyes warned that he might want her to sing for her supper.

'How very kind,' she said, and blamed the fact of Stein sitting behind her, and her awareness of him, that she could not come up with a better excuse than, 'but it is rather short notice.'

'Oh.' There was a wealth of disappointment in the sound. But while Zarah was trying to think up some excuse should Rolv suggest some other time, he had put his disappointment from him, to dangle the most enticing of baits. 'I have discovered a little more of Fru Kildedalen's other friend—the one who went with my mother to visit her when she came to Dalvik that first time,' he said. 'I thought perhaps you might be interested.'

'You . . .' sprang from her before she could control it. Control, and awareness of Stein and how she could not speak freely in front of him on this subject, arrived together. A second later she knew it would be much better to talk on this subject that interested her most, not only away from Stein, but away from the house altogether. Hurriedly she changed that 'You . . .' into, 'You'll call for me?'

His reply was prompt. 'Shall I call at thirty minutes past seven o'clock?'

'Seven-thirty will be fine,' she told him, then she said goodbye and put down the phone.

About to leave the room, she flicked a glance at Stein. Why his expression should be as black as thunder was beyond her, but as that imp of mischief she had experienced before again surged up, she cared not what expression he wore.

'In case you didn't hear,' she offered sarcastically, 'I won't be in to dinner tonight.'

Icy grey eyes bored into defiant brown ones. Zarah anticipated a reply along the lines of Stein giving three hearty cheers that she would not be at the same table as him that night. But his reply was nothing of the sort, but was a coldly gritted:

'Might I know the name of the man you've invited into my father's home?'

Anger flared in her. It was only his protection of his father which made him ask the question, she knew that, but it annoyed her just the same. Was she likely to bring anyone into the home who might be insensitive to his father's suffering? Rolv himself had observed that Haldor did not know where he was. That in itself decreed that Rolv must have some depth of sensitivity. Pride dug itself in, and right then Zarah decided—even if she had to sit on the doorstep to wait for Rolv—that she would not invite him indoors.

'His name,' she said coolly, 'is Rolv Fjeld.'

'The man with the boat hire business,' he rapped, and before she could so much as nod her head, 'Where did you meet him?' he barked.

'At his boatyard—where else?' snapped Zarah, and marched angrily from the study, to bump into Fru Onsvag. Rapidly she had to try to cool down, as she endeavoured to convey to the housekeeper that she would not require a meal that night.

At seven-fifteen, Zarah left her room and went to wait downstairs for Rolv Fjeld. Her thoughts were centred on how in the next few hours she could have progressed one step nearer her goal, when Stein came down the stairs and spotted her standing around in the hall. Their eyes met, but she had nothing she wanted to say to him—that was, until she saw his mouth tighten, and knew he had registered that the amber dress she wore was another of her more-expensive-than-most numbers—an expensive number he had paid for. Her pride buffeted, she had no defence but to put up a show of not caring a damn.

'Don't wait up,' she tossed at him airily, only to earn herself another helping of his aggression.

'*Don't you*——' he snarled, 'be late back!' About to tell him what he could do with his orders, Zarah was promptly flattened when Stein followed up his command with, 'It takes my father an age to get off to sleep. What he doesn't need, when finally he has fallen asleep, is to be awakened in the early hours by the slamming of car doors!'

With that he strode off, and Zarah made the sudden discovery that she did not like fighting with him! Needing some air, she went to wait outside.

By the time she saw Rolv Fjeld steer his car up the drive, she had got herself back together again. She cared not a hoot then if she and Stein had to slug it out for evermore. It came more naturally to her to be friendy, so what must have attacked her a short while ago must have been nothing but her basic instinct not to fight. She pushed away a memory of Stein, his lips gentle over hers, and knew that they would never be friends. Which, since she was not the type to let anyone sit on her, forced her to accept that enemies were what she and Stein would always be.

'You look charming,' Rolv complimented her when she slid into the passenger seat.

Zarah found a smile and guessed, in the half-hour drive which followed, that Rolv must have consulted his English dictionary for words of flattery. He took her to a smart hotel outside Dalvik, and as the evening advanced, his compliments were many.

Not one word, though, did he say about the only reason she had accepted his invitation anyway. In her anxiety that he should not see how important his information was to her, Zarah encouraged him to talk about his boatyard and anything else impersonal she could think of.

When the time came for the waiter to consult them on what they wanted for dessert, however, and then went to attend to their order, she just could not hold back any longer.

'Oh—by the way,' she said, as if she had only then remembered, 'you said something about knowing a little more of my aunt's other friend . . .'

'Ah, yes,' he smiled, but confessed, 'it is really not so much.'

Sensing she was doomed for disappointment, Zarah still wanted to hear what he had learned, however small. 'But,' she pressed, as casually as she was able, 'you have discovered something?'

'From my sister,' he revealed. 'Leikny and her husband are to go on a month's holiday in Spain tomorrow, so Leikny came to see me yesterday.'

'To say goodbye?' Zarah pushed him on.

He shook his head and, looking sorry for himself, explained, 'Leikny has always been a—boss sister, and is also what I think you call a "good-doer". The trouble with good-doers,' he sighed, 'is when they—er—lasso you in to help their good works.'

What this had got to do with her aunt's friend of the old days, Zarah could not see. But, patient this long, she tried to keep patience a little longer. 'Your sister has roped you in to help with some good cause?' she prompted.

'Leikny lives in Oslo,' he yielded, 'and in her voluntary work at a hospital for permanent patients, she has found some old woman who she insists is some obscure relative of ours. This woman never has any visitors, so it is my sister's nature that she must visit the hospital every Sunday afternoon. Leikny's good works,' Rolv heaved another sigh, 'became my good works when she refused to leave until she had my promise that I would do—what she said is only my duty to a relative—and visit the old woman each Sunday while she is away.'

His expression endorsed his lack of inclination to do his duty, and might have appeared droll to Zarah had she not been growing more and more impatient at the time it was taking him to tell her what she was there to hear.

'You'll probably feel a warm glow to have cheered the week of a hospital-bound elderly lady,' she murmured.

'I can think of something better to do with my next four Sundays than drive to Oslo,' he told her suggestively.

'This lady,' Zarah said quickly, 'is she the one who was friends with my aunt?'

'No,' Rolv replied, but he was back on the course Zarah wanted, when he added, 'I was telling my sister how you had asked me the way to the cemetery, and how we had been talking of Fru Kildedalen, and straight off her tongue, Leikny said, "I remember Fru Kildedalen from years ago. I was with Mother when she and Fru Wenstad went to the little house to wish her welcome to Norway."

It seemed to have taken light years to get the name 'Fru Wenstad' out of him. But Zarah wanted more. 'What else did your sister say?' she asked.

'About Fru Wenstad?' Zarah nodded. 'Nothing more, I think,' he said disappointingly. 'From there, Leikny remembered how Fru Wenstad had a dog with only three legs, but as I started to reminisce, she was determined to tell me of the old lady in Oslo who she could not bear to think of having no visitors until she returned from holiday. Then Leikny went on and on, until I was worn down into agreeing that I could not let her holiday be ruined. She left when I gave her my promise.'

'You'll keep your promise, of course,' Zarah murmured, doing her best to look sympathetic to his plight.

'Leikny wouldn't never let me forget it if I did not,' Rolv grumbled. 'She would mention it at every meeting, and every telephone call, until the day I die.' Suddenly he brightened. 'But that is enough about my sister. Let us talk of you.'

The waiter arrived with the desserts they had ordered, and Rolv did his best to draw Zarah out as they ate. But her mind was only half with him, for she was searching for some seemingly trivial way to bring the conversation back to Fru Wenstad. Try as she might, however, they had reached the coffee stage, and still she had no words that would show him how important Fru Wenstad was to her.

'You have enjoyed your meal?' Rolv enquired with a flash of his teeth when he had settled the bill.

'Very much,' she replied, with visions of calling on Fru Wenstad first thing tomorrow.

'Good,' he smiled. 'Now I think we shall go to the dance.'

'Dance?' she exclaimed.

'You do not wish to dance?' His smile was exchanged for a hurt look.

'It isn't that I don't want to go dancing with you,' Zarah, who had an aversion to telling lies, lied unblushingly, 'it's just that, with my uncle's house still in mourning,' she brought out of the hat, 'it doesn't seem— er—quite right that I should . . .' She had no need to continue. Rolv had shown a basic goodness, for all his grumbles, in the way he had given his sister his promise rather than ruin her holiday. That same basic goodness was there when he immediately understood.

'Then I shall return you to your uncle's house,' he said.

Zarah spent most of the drive back to Dalvik in parrying Rolv's warm overtures, and in trying still to find an opportunity to bring up Fru Wenstad's name. They were nearly at the house when, in fear that he might drive off and she would still not know the good lady's address, suddenly she blurted out:

'I expect Fru Wenstad still lives in Dalvik?'

'I would know if she did,' Rolv said amiably, and seemed to think it simply a peculiarity of the English to blurt out sudden questions à propos nothing. 'Everyone knows everyone around here,' he remarked as he turned the car into the Kildedalen drive.

'Are you saying that she no longer lives in Dalvik?'

'She moved away many years ago,' he replied, and halted the car at the house. Zarah, hiding her disappointment, and with no wish for him to try to kiss her good night, promptly got out of the car.

Her intention to thank him politely for taking her out to dinner and to quietly close the door was forestalled when Rolv too left the car and came to place an arm about her shoulders. Zarah moved to the front door. Rolv went with her.

'Thank you for a very nice evening,' she said pleasantly, and reached down for the door knob.

'When shall I see you again?' he asked. 'Tomorrow . . .'

'I don't think, in the circumstances,' she interrupted quickly, 'that it would be respectful to my uncle if I went out too frequently.'

'How sweet and thoughtful you are!' said Rolv warmly. 'Perhaps I might telephone you to make some arrangement?' Zarah hesitated to give him that encouragement, and coaxingly he suggested, 'If you wish, I can make few enquiries to see if I can find out where Fru Wenstad now resides?'

Zarah had the uncomfortable feeling that Rolv was a shade more perceptive than she had thought, but even so, she had to answer, 'I should—like you to do that.' His arm tightening about her shoulders told her it was time to test the door knob.

Her fear that Stein might have locked her out was discarded when the door gave inwards and a shaft of light from a left-on lamp penetrated the outside semi-darkness. Without apparent haste, Zarah moved until Rolv's arm had fallen away and she was on one side of the slightly ajar door and he was on the other.

'Good night,' she bade him, and when his expression showed that this was not the way he had meant the evening to end, 'I'll look forward to your phone call,' she smiled, and closed the door.

Her thoughts on what chance there was of him finding out Fru Wenstad's address, Zarah turned from the door to see Stein standing there watching her. His grim expression had nothing at all to do with his having just overheard her tell Rolv that she would look forward to his phone call, she knew that. Just as she knew that odd feeling of not wanting to fight with him had only been momentary. Truly, Stein Kildedalen brought out the worst in her!

She moved, meaning to pass him without comment, but was along on a level with him when she remembered his snarled *'Don't you*—be late back!'

'There you are, you see,' she said sweetly, finding it absolutely beyond her capabilities not to make some remark, 'home before midnight.'

His harsh retort of, *'Your* home is in England,' stopped

her dead in her tracks. It hurt. And, hurt, Zarah took less than a second to toss back the retort she thought would needle him most.

'Not for another five and a bit months, it isn't!' she snapped, and saw from the blaze of anger in his eyes that she had indeed needled him.

'You refuse to go?' he challenged angrily.

Hurt dug deeper. 'What . . .' she scoffed, '. . .and lose my right to those shares?'

To be reminded of those shares had not charmed him, she observed: the darkening of his expression told her that much. And that was before, to reveal he had not forgotten her previously stated view that she would be a fool to part with those shares when they were going up in value the whole time, he fired:

'I'll give you the market value six months hence. Agree to go, and I'll give you a written undertaking to the effect . . .'

'Save your ink!' flared Zarah on an uprush of wounded feeling, then she stamped down her emotion to needle some more. 'Your father himself,' she reminded him with a return of her sweet tone, 'told me that this is my home now.'

'God in heaven,' Stein seethed, 'you're not intending to stay longer than six months!'

She smiled. 'I—might,' she purred, 'I just might.' But the glimpse she caught of his hands clenching and unclenching was sufficient to make her decide to go to bed. She went quickly.

Zarah kept out of Stein's way as much as possible in the week that followed. She found it disturbed her that anyone should dislike her to the extent that he did. Though since she disliked him with an equal intensity, she supposed she had nothing to grumble about. That being the case, it was something of a puzzle, still, why his

unveiled hint that he wanted her to leave should have
hurt her the way it had.

By the end of the week Zarah had recovered her
equilibrium, and was certain she did not give a damn
what he said. Tough luck, Stein, she thought. It's your
father's house, not yours, and I'm your father's guest.

It had been a bad week none the less. She had taken
over in the kitchen again on Thursday, and Stein had
again washed the dishes after the evening meal, but the
way they would pass each other without a word was, by
then, the least of her troubles. She had not believed she
had placed all that much faith in Rolv Fjeld being able to
come up with Fru Wenstad's address. But when no call
came from him, her feeling of despondency made her
realise that, deep down, she must have done. And to cap
it all, the weather had changed.

She was still taking her daily constitutional in the faint
hope that she might bump into someone who had known
her aunt before she had become Haldor's bride. But as
Zarah looked at the overcast skies on Saturday afternoon, it was touch and go whether she gave it a miss. Her
inner unrest settled the matter. She donned her raincoat,
just in case, and went out.

Her feet were soon taking her a way she seldom went,
but which was the route she had taken that day she had
asked Rolv for directions. Not that she was going to walk
that far today. Zarah had no wish to be a fair sprint from
home should the heavens open.

Even so, with the rain keeping off, she walked further
than she had intended. She was just thinking of going
back when she saw a car that looked familiar coming
towards her. A second later she recognised the car as the
one she had been in with Rolv Fjeld.

Suddenly she realised that, if Rolv stopped, she would
have a splendid opportunity to remind him that he had

been going to make enquiries about Fru Wenstad's address.

Rolv did stop, his smile flashing out when he left his car and came over to her. 'I hoped I would meet you,' he said, which Zarah would have taken with a pinch of salt, but he added, 'I telephoned you a few minutes ago, but Stein Kildedalen—in a bad humour, I think, from the way he spoke—told me that you were out.'

'I like to take a walk each day,' Zarah informed him.

'It is the same with us Norwegians,' he replied. 'We love to be out in the open air.' Again he smiled, but as she felt reluctant to ask why he had telephoned lest it had been merely to ask her for another date, she said nothing. He then extracted a piece of paper from his pocket and handed it to her. 'Fru Wenstad's address.' he beamed.

'Fru . . .' Suddenly Zarah was beaming too. Before she could get the words out to thank him, however, another car she recognised came into her line of vision. The smile of pleasure was still on her face when Stein looked at her, looked through her, and, his expression thunderous, drove on.

'I have worked all this week trying to get the address for you,' Rolv told her, while Zarah noted that the address he had given her was somewhere in Oslo.

'Thank you,' she smiled. 'You've been more than kind. I shall now be able to write to Fru Wenstad to—er—introduce myself.'

'You could introduce yourself to her in person tomorrow, if you wish,' Rolv stated quickly.

Zarah managed to hide the rush of emotion that idea generated, and enquired, more calmly than she felt, 'Fru Wenstad is coming to Dalvik tomorrow?'

He shook his head. 'You have forgotten,' he said ruefully. 'I still have another three Sunday visits to make to one of my sister's good works. I am going to Oslo tomorrow. It would be my pleasure to take you with me, and to bring you back.'

The urge to go with him and not to wait for any letter she wrote to reach Fru Wenstad, and then to have to have to watch impatiently every day for a reply, would not be denied.

'Would you?' she asked, trying to hide her eagerness not to wait a moment longer than she had to.

'Of course,' he answered. But all at once Zarah became aware of something in his eyes that made her feel a trifle uneasy.

'You'll—er—be coming back to Dalvik tomorrow night?' she thought to enquire.

'I did not return until Monday, last weekend,' he told her. 'Leikny,' he went on, 'has told me to use her house in her absence.' That sounded straightforward enough, and the obvious thing for him to do if he did not want to drive to Oslo and back the same day. But Zarah knew she had been right to be wary, when casually, too casually, he let fall, 'There is room in Leikny's house for you also to stay.'

Every instinct told Zarah that this was where she advised him that she would stick to her original idea, and would write to Fru Wenstad. Against that, though, was this restlessness within her. She wanted peace from those thoughts, those questions, that tormented. She had to go with him—she could not wait.

'It's sweet of you to offer, but I think I'll book into a hotel,' she accepted his invitation of transport only.

Rolv smiled, and now the matter was settled satisfactorily as far as she was concerned, Zarah had no obstacle to put in the way when he said, 'I like to leave early.'

'I'll be ready at whatever time you say,' she smiled.

'Then I shall call for you at six o'clock.'

Six o'clock was indeed early, but having told him she would be ready at whatever time, Zarah saw little point in suggesting a later hour. She left him, declining a lift back to the house by reminding him that she was out for a walk, and went on her way with mixed feelings.

By the time she had reached the house, though, any worries that Rolv might prove amorously tiresome had been pushed aside. She had remembered the basic goodness she had witnessed in him, and was sure he would not be too difficult to handle. But, in any case, the thought that by this time tomorrow she could know for certain whose daughter she was far outweighed any disquiet about him.

She was in her room going over everything for the umpteenth time, when suddenly something she had not so far thought of popped into her head. How was she to explain her absence to Haldor?

Courtesy, if not the affection she had for him, demanded that she tell him something, but what? No way could she tell him the truth. Just a hint that she was going to Oslo to look up an old acquaintance of his wife, would be more than enough for him to want to know more.

From then until it was time to go down to dinner, Zarah chewed the matter over. But she was still far from happy when she left her room to go to the dining room,.

'Good evening,' she said generally to the two present, and took her usual seat, to make another discovery. It was all very well to rehearse what she was going to say to Haldor while up in her room, but she discovered that she had a very definite reluctance to tell him anything in front of his cold-eyed son.

Which was perhaps why her tongue stuck to her palate each time she was about to get the words out. When Fru Onsvag came in with the dessert, Zarah knew she could delay no longer. Soon Haldor would disappear into his private sanctum, and it would be too late.

She picked up her spoon, ready to dip it into her orange syllabub. 'Oh, by the way, Uncle Haldor,' she said, ignoring Stein, 'I'm going to Oslo tomorrow.'

Haldor took his uninterested gaze from his dessert. 'You're going—to Oslo?' he queried blankly.

'I thought it was about time I took in a little sightseeing,' she told him with a gentle smile. A lie had been necessary if she was not to upset him more than he was upset already. But, when she had found it difficult to lie to him, she could have done without Stein chipping in with his twopennyworth.

'How, might one enquire,' he drawled, when she hadn't been speaking to him, 'do you propose getting to Oslo?'

From choice, Zarah would have preferred to go on ignoring Stein, but, for his father's sake, she had to answer Stein. 'Actually,' she said, observing his 'no love lost' look, 'Rolv Fjeld has business in Oslo—he's offered to give me a lift.'

The furious expression that crossed Stein's face as he heard whom she was going with caused Zarah to glance elsewhere. Why he should look ready to erupt, she had no idea. But, expecting to have a few short and sharp words assualt her ears at any second, she was doubly startled when, although sharp words did hit her ears, they did not come from Stein—but from his father!

His, 'You will come back to us, Zarah?' was so unlike any tone she had ever heard from him that to hear him speak so, with authority, with life in his voice, made her stare at him. Beneath that alive tone, though, she realised suddenly, was an underlying note of anxiety, in case she did not come back!

'I'd like to come back, if that's all right with you,' she answered, her heart going out to him.

Her reply was all he wanted to hear, apparently.

Because although he did not say effusively that it was what he wanted, his nod, the semblance of a relieved smile that nearly made a full smile made Zarah feel she was a welcome guest. Haldor took up his spoon and dipped it into the syllabub in front of him. Zarah was just about to do the same with her sweet when, abruptly, Stein questioned:

'You will return tomorrow evening?'

Her relief to be satisfactorily over the hurdle of explaining her intended absence to Haldor was short-lived. Trust Stein to have more interest in the nitty-gritty of her plans! Why, when it would make him ecstatic if she didn't return at all, couldn't he take more interest in his food? She wanted to tell him to run for an answer. But, again so Haldor would think everything was sweetness and light between her and his son, she was forced to reply.

'As a matter of fact,' she flicked Stein a glance, 'I was thinking of staying in Oslo until Monday.' Deliberately she had made her voice light, but there was no corresponding lightness in Stein's voice when he grated aggressively;

'Fjeld, I assume, will be on hand to give you a lift back to Dalvik too?'

His aggressive tone annoyed her. Even when she did not want it to annoy her, it still did. 'You assume correctly,' she snapped, then had to swallow down her ire as Haldor looked at her curiously. 'Stein,' she tacked on pleasantly.

The rest of the meal, which to her relief took only a few minutes, was finished in silence. Stein had nothing more to say, but she knew, and hated him for it, that he was thinking a lot. He had seen her just as Rolv had given her the news that he knew the whereabouts of Fru Wenstad. He had seen her beaming her head off at Rolv.

Remembering the way Stein so continually put two and two together to make five where she was concerned, Zarah knew he had done it again. Without question, Stein was positive that she and Rolv Fjeld were going to Oslo together tomorrow for purposes that had nothing at all to do with sightseeing!

CHAPTER SEVEN

THE next morning, feeling knotted up inside from what she might hear from Fru Wenstad, Zarah was glad of Rolv Fjeld's chatter that needed only the occasional reply. After about an hour, though, his conversation began to wane, and as another hour went by, her inner turmoil increased.

They were driving through an area where tall pine trees were interspersed with fields of golden corn, when Zarah realised she should have written or have telephoned. She had been in her room after dinner last night when she had first thought of telephoning Fru Wenstad to ask if it was convenient to call and see her today. Against that, though, was the knowledge that she would have to ask Stein for the Oslo telephone directory. Stein was very definitely not her favourite person just then. She had no wish to have to do battle with him should he become obstructive and ask her what she wanted the directory for.

They were on the outskirts of Oslo when Zarah switched her thoughts from what she should have done to what she should be doing. What she should be doing was to think up some tactful way of telling Rolv that she would prefer to see Fru Wenstad alone.

The nearer they got to Oslo, the more agitated did Zarah become. When Rolv turned off the major road, drove on for some minutes, and then stopped at a neat timber-framed house, her tension grew.

'Is—this where Fru Wenstad lives?' she asked quickly, agitated that he looked to be getting out of the car to go to the door with her.

'It is where my sister lives,' grinned Rolv. 'It has been a long drive,' he added as he vacated the driving seat, 'I wish for a cup of coffee.'

Zarah stamped down her need to get her meeting with Fru Wenstad over, and got out of the car too. Rolv had been kindness itself to bring her, and had been at the wheel of his car for almost four hours. No wonder he wanted some refreshment! She decided as they entered the house, that perhaps ten o'clock in the morning was a little early to descend on Fru Wenstad.

She was as tense as ever, though, when at Rolv's 'Come and talk to me in the kitchen,' she went and stood by while he boiled up a kettle and took out a couple of cups and saucers.

His supply of inconsequential chat was once more inexhaustible as he spooned coffee into cups and opened the milk he had brought with him. Beginning to feel the strain, Zarah thought her replies were not brilliant conversation pieces either.

They had moved to a tastefully furnished sitting room, when she discovered that Rolv had seen through her monosyllabic answers to note the inner tension she was under. What shook her more, though, was that he seemed to think it was in his power to produce a cure.

She was sat beside him on the settee, with a cup and saucer in one hand, when, without warning, his arm came about her shoulders. Abruptly she moved to get free, her eyes jerking to his.

'You wish to finish your coffee first?' he asked reproachfully.

'First?' queried Zarah—stupidly, she realised later.

'My lovemaking will make you relax,' he promised, and smiled.

In an instant her coffee was put down and Zarah was on her feet. 'Lovemaking!' she echoed.

His smile departed, and he was on his feet too when,

mystified by her astonishment, he queried, 'You are playing with me? You wish me to make love with you, but you wish to make games with me first.'

'I do *not* wish to make love with you,' Zarah took a step away to tell him severely, 'or to play games. I don't know what . . .'

'It is an English joke?' he butted in, puzzled.

'It is no joke,' she said repressively.

'But . . .' For a moment he seemed dumbfounded and stuck for words. 'But,' he repeated, 'how can you agree to spend the night with me, and not intend to make love?'

'I never agreed to spend the night with you!' Zarah protested, amazed. 'I told you I'd book into a hotel.'

'But you *must* know it is impossible to find a hotel room in Oslo this weekend!' he exclaimed. 'Everyone knows that, as well as normal hotel bookings, the three different exhibitions which are on in the capital have made certain that no one will get a room unless they have reserved much in advance.'

'*I* didn't know.' she said faintly. Then, uncertain, although he looked sincere, if he was telling the truth, or if he had just made it up, she told him, 'I'd better go.'

'Go!'

His exclamation, together with his incredulous expression, told her that he was still not entirely convinced that this was not some kind of English joke. 'Thank you for giving me a lift this far,' she said, and realising that now she had ruined his plans for a cosy overnight stop for two, she could now whistle for a lift any further, she made for the door.

She had, however, forgotten the basic goodness she had previously credited him with. For, regardless of any sore feelings he might have, as she opened the door, his better self surfaced.

'I cannot leave you to take a lift with anyone you do not know,' he sighed. 'I will take you into the city.'

Conscious that some of his usual good humour had deserted him, Zarah fully expected Rolv to dump her somewhere in the middle of Oslo. To her surprise, though, he showed he had not forgotten her wish to see Fru Wenstad, and halted his car not in the city centre, but in an area where an old building had been made over into an apartment block.

'I thought you might want to visit Fru Wenstad before you start to look for a hotel room,' he explained. And while Zarah felt knotted up inside again to realise that in a very few minutes her quest could be over, he wrote something down on a piece of paper. His good humour appeared to have fully returned when, his familiar grin back in place, he handed her what he had written, and suggested confidently, 'When you find you have nowhere to stay, either telephone me to come for you, or take a taxi to Leikny's address.'

She took the piece of paper from him and pushed it into her raincoat pocket, but she had to smile as she told him, 'You don't give up, do you?' Then she reached for the overnight bag on the back seat and stepped out into pouring rain. With a cheery wave, Rolve drove off. Promptly Zarah forgot him.

Oblivious of the downpour, she had no need to refer to the other piece of paper which Rolve had given her yesterday. Fru Wenstad's address was burned in her brain.

The outside door which would lead to flat 2A was a few steps from the kerb. Zarah quickly spotted the line of door bells, but had to take a deep and steadying breath before she pressed the one marked '2A'.

She pressed it again after several minutes had gone by and no one answered. Unable to accept that Fru Wenstad was not at home, when no sound was heard from within, Zarah pressed the bell a long third time. Then she tested the door. It was locked.

She checked her watch, and saw that it had gone eleven. Perhaps Fru Wenstad had gone to church? What if she was out for the day? Zarah pressed the bell once more before, reluctantly, she gave up.

She had been walking without sense of direction when she realised that she was getting soaked, and had better shelter in a doorway while she decided what to do.

When the rain fined down to a drizzle, Zarah left her shelter and, staying in the vicinity, she walked around until midday. Then she went back to try the bell of '2A' once more. Again there was no answer.

This time, when she left the solid outside door, Zarah ventured further. Her initial thought was to return every hour, her next thought was that if Rolv's warning about the scarcity of hotel accommodation was accurate, then she had better do something about finding a room for the night.

Though since a hotel would probably cost the earth, she decided to track down the tourist information office. They would be bound to know of some inexpensive *pensjonat* where she might lay her head that night.

An hour later, she found herself in Karl Johans Gate, a long, long street which, despite the rain, had much pedestrian traffic. She chanced asking directions to the tourist information office, and discovered she had hit upon someone else who could speak English, when the lady pointed the way, and told her it was not far.

Zarah had by then formed the impression that Oslo seemed closed for the day, but she was crossing into Rosenkrantz Gate when she spotted a restaurant by the name of Southern Fried Chicken that was open. More to get in out of the rain than anything else, she went in and ordered a coffee.

She took her coffee to a table near to the open door, where a steady stream of like-minded tourists dived in out of the rain. A glance at her watch showed it had gone half past one, and while she knew she should be making for the tourist information office and be getting on with securing a room for the night it was tempting to stay inside out of the wet and not move.

She did move, though. Though perhaps 'jump' was a more apt description. For, deep in thought, her mind again on what Fru Wenstad might tell her, she suddenly heard a voice, a voice she knew, break into her thoughts to ask:

'Sheltering from the rain?'

Her head jerked up. For a moment as she recognised a rain-coated Stein Kildedalen, who should by rights be in Dalvik, a four-hour drive away, and not in Oslo, she was incapable of speech. 'What . . .' she gasped. 'Where did . . .' she tried, and as her heart started to beat energetically, and she was suddenly aware of what a wreck she must look, she found she was having to concentrate really hard to form one single solitary sentence. Stein had taken the seat opposite her by the time she had got enough wind to accuse, 'You *followed* me!'

'I should be up so early?' Stein neatly sidestepped her accusation, and in doing so reminded her of the way she had 'forgotten' to tell anyone of her six o'clock start.

But Zarah was starting to recover her wits, and she was sure then that if he had not exactly tailed Rolv's car all the way from Dalvik, he *had* followed her.

'You didn't say you were coming to Oslo when I told you my plans last night,' she looked him straight in the eye to state.

Stein stared levelly back. Then slowly revealed, 'I didn't—appreciate, until my father and I were at breakfast—and you weren't—how concerned he was about you.'

'Your father's con . . .' Zarah broke off. 'You've left him by himself!' she realised suddenly, *her* concern for

Haldor unmistakable. 'You've . . .' Again she broke off. Stein was smiling. He was actually smiling—at her! The mouth that had once kissed hers was actually . . .

'You've no cause to worry,'he murmured. 'A widower friend of my father is keen to buy his boat, and arrived as I left. Herr Juvkam,' he added, a smile still there in his eyes, 'will spend the day with him.'

Taken aback that Stein had just credited her with a capability to worry over anyone but herself, Zarah did her best to assimilate what else he had just said. But the fact that there was a seldom-seen curve to his mouth when he was talking to her had created the most peculiar sensation inside her.

'Er—Uncle Haldor—your father,' she did her best to overcome that sensation, 'he—er—asked you to come after me?' She got herself more of one piece, and was then able to add, 'You might not have found me.'

Any sign of a smile promptly disappeared, and to Zarah's mind Stein was soon back to being his tough arrogant self, when he told her, 'I knew you'd made it as far as Oslo.'

'How could you know?' she challenged, certain she didn't give a damn if he never smiled again. At pains to let him know he was not so smart as he thought he was, she spoke entirely without thinking, when she burst out, 'You'd never have come across me had things gone the way Rolv Fjeld thought they would. If . . .' Abruptly, she broke off.

'If things had gone the way Fjeld had planned,' Stein did not hesitate to finish for her, 'you'd have stayed the night, not in a hotel, but in Leikny Moreite's home—with him.'

'How do you know that?' Stein's acuteness left her gasping.

'Leikny told me she was about to go on holiday when I bumped into her in Dalvik the other week,' Stein shrugged. 'I followed my nose, looked up her address, and called there first.'

Clever devil, Zarah thought, beginning to feel feather-brained. 'You saw Rolv?' she questioned, and at his confirming nod, great alarm bells suddenly started to go off. What if Rolv had told him about her wish to see Fru Wenstad? What if he had told him that he had delivered her to Fru Wenstad's home? 'Rolv,' she said hurriedly, 'he—er . . .' she slowed down, 'he's probably told you how he dropped me off in Oslo, to—er . . .'

'To find a hotel room—*for one*.'

Zarah had no objection to Stein finishing the sentence for her this time. But the emphasis he had put on the words '*for one*' made her mutter, 'I knew you thought I was going off with him for . . . Well, anyway,' she amended, finding she was getting herself in something of a pickle, 'you should have believed me when I told you I wanted to do some sightseeing.'

She followed his glance to the downpour still going on outside, but although she told herself she was quite cross with him, she almost erupted into laughter when he muttered, 'You've chosen a fine day for it.' There was no sign of humour in him, she saw, for his expression was stern, and any laughter in her promptly disappeared, when he bit harshly, 'Are you so naïve, woman, that you'd no idea Fjeld's plan of an overnight stop was never that you should sleep anywhere but with him?'

'Of course I'm not' she flared, but lowered her voice when she suddenly became aware of the curious stares from a couple at the next table. 'What does it matter anyway?' she hissed. 'Rolv soon got the message that I don't go in for sleeping around.'

Again she had spoken without thinking first. She saw Stein's brow shoot up, but she could cheerfully have murdered him when, without following suit and lowering his voice, he asked astoundedly 'You're a *virgin*?'

Another glance flicked at the couple with the ringside seat showed that they were growing more intrigued by the minute. 'Let all Oslo know!' Zarah erupted, angrier than ever when, obviously realising from her reply that she was indeed a virgin, Stein swore—she was positive—in Norwegian, then blasted her:

'My God, you're not safe out . . .'

'Shut up!' Zarah ground out through gritted teeth, not caring whether his thunderstruck expression came from the fact of it sinking in that she was a virgin, or from the fact that she had just publicly told him to shut up. In any event, he would *not* shut up.

'You crazy idiot!' he rounded on her. 'Didn't you see the sort of man Fjeld is? Didn't it dawn on you that if he refused to take "no" for an answer, you could have been . . .' Words seemed to fail him, but not for very long. 'God in heaven,' he exploded, 'in all likelihood, Fjeld is only waiting for you to run into difficulty trying to get a hotel room—then he'll pounce!' Stein's jaw was jutting at an aggressive angle. 'He's expecting you to ring him, isn't he?' he asked toughly.

With Rolv's sister's address and telephone number in her pocket, Zarah had no defence. But she did not need one. She had it with Stein Kildedalen anyway. In one movement she had scooped up her overnight bag and was making a beeline out of the restaurant.

Furious with him that he should take it upon himself to harangue her in public—even if she had publicly told him to 'shut up' first—when he knew as well as she did that nearly everyone in Norway spoke English, Zarah stormed on.

Without heeding where she was going, more by luck than by judgement, she found that she had marched down the street, crossed the road and had turned the corner to find herself near the entrance to the City Hall where the tourist information office was.

She had just made up her mind to go in, when the owner of a pair of footsteps behind drew level. She knew she had not shaken off Stein when a hand reached down and took her overnight bag form her.

Her lips compressed, she stopped dead. A few uncomplimentary names rose to her tongue, then suddenly, to her right, she saw that a tour coach was about to depart. The only thought in her head then was to get free of Stein.

Without stopping to consider that since he had hold of her overnight bag she did not have so much as a toothbrush, Zarah took off at a sprint. She made it just as the automatic doors were about to close, and the bus moved off.

Pleased with herself, she was just going to sink into the only double seat left, when she became aware that she was not the last person to enter the bus.

'I'll put your bag up here, shall I?' Stein asked pleasantly. He accepted her icy glare as a 'Yes, please', and stowed her bag aloft, then took the seat next to her.

It would have been undignified, she decided when someone came to collect their fares, to scream at the top of her lungs that she wanted to pay her own fare, so she looked out of the window while Stein forked out for two tickets.

Intent on ignoring him, she was concentrating her attention on pretending to look out of the misted up windows when Stein enquired mildly:

'Incidentally, did you manage to find a hotel room?'

'Be quiet!' she tossed over her shoulder.

'Which means you haven't,' he murmured.

'Why else would I tote my overnight bag around?' she snapped

'Why else?' he agreed.

Zarah decided to say not another word to him. But although she tried to get interested in what the tour guide was saying, she had to own that with Stein sitting next to her, she was finding her interest was not what it should have been. The reason for that was plain, though. Never in a month of Sundays would she ever have dreamed that the day would come when she and Stein would sit side by side on a tour bus. Pigs would fly, she would have thought, before Stein would smile at her. Yet here they were on a tour bus, and he had not only smiled but, if her vibes were accurate, he was behaving far less disagreeably than he had ever done before.

The first stop on the tour was a visit to the Viking Ship Museum. Stein kept alongside her as their guide led them to a large hall that housed historic wooden vessels that had lain buried for hundreds of years until they were excavated.

Zarah started to feel uneasy when he stuck to her side as she walked the length of the hall. Though since her only escape was back to the coach, when he would doubtless come and sit beside her, she saw little point in trying to duck away from him.

The next port of call was to a folk museum and a stave church. But Zarah had started to worry, and could not lose herself in the folk art and handicrafts. Stein had gone with her every step of the way, and in her view he was taking his duty to his father much too far. Fair enough, Stein was only here because of the concern Haldor must have shown at breakfast, but if they went on like this, Stein might take it into his head to accompany her when the tour was over!

Their next stop was to see the Polar exploration ship *Fram*, in which Fridtjof Nansen had reached further north than anyone before. *Fram* had later been used by Roald Amundsen on his expedition to the South Pole, Zarah learned, but all the while her niggle of worry was growing.

When the tour was over, she wanted to make another

visit to Fru Wenstad's apartment. But how could she do
that if Stein insisted on dogging her heels?

When they arrived at the last item on the agenda,
Zarah had worked herself up into a fine state of being
certain she was never going to be able to give Stein the
slip. When at any other time she would have been
overawed to see the frail-looking Kon-Tiki raft in which
Thor Heyerdahl with five companions had drifted
thousands of miles across the Pacific, she was in
consequence more hot and bothered about Stein.

The sky was still overcast when the coach returned to
Oslo, but that it had stopped raining was the only bright
spot, in Zarah's opinion.

'I enjoyed that,' she made the effort to say, and even
smiled at Stein as she stood with him outside the City
Hall. 'Thank you for your company,' she said with the
biggest hint she could find that his company was no
longer required. As an extra hint, she went to take her
overnight bag from him. But swine that he was, he hung
on to it.

'Where to now?' he asked pleasantly.

Zarah held on to her smile—just. 'You must want to
get home,' she suggested.

Stein smiled too, and she had the oddest notion that he
was playing her at her own game. Whatever game he was
playing, though, it was not being played the way she
wanted it, when he replied smoothly:

'For my father's peace of mind, I'll first find you a
hotel room.' About to tell him she would find her own
hotel room, Zarah was left without any choice when he
took a firm grip on her arm, and with a pleasant, 'My
car's not far away,' marched her off to where he had
parked his car.

By the time they were driving along, however, Zarah
had simmered down from her anger at his high-handed
treatment. By then she had realised that to go along with

him might be the better option. Once he had made sure of her overnight accommodation, she reasoned, he would return to Dalvik, and she, free from the fear of having him breathing down her neck, would be able to hotfoot it round to see Fru Wenstad.

That was her reasoning before Stein drove his car to the car park at the rear of what must be one of the smartest hotels in Oslo. Panic that it would cost an arm and a leg to stay there had set in when he escorted her inside to the plush reception area. In view of their previous battles when the subject of money had come up, though, pride prevented her from telling him she could not afford such luxury. She wasn't going to have him think she was fishing for him to pay her hotel bill.

She hoped against hope that the hotel was full. But as she stood beside him and saw that the receptionist was reaching for a registration card, so her hope died.

When, either accidentally or on purpose, the young woman handed him not one registration document but two, Zarah felt panic of another sort.

In her alarm, she was incapable of clear thought. With hunted eyes she looked towards the front exit. All she could think then was that Stein intended to stay at the hotel too, and that she would *never* be free of him to make her solo visit to see Fru Wenstad. The fact that he had parked his car at the rear, instead of using a short-term parking spot out front—like that taxi had which had just pulled up—seemed to confirm it.

She had been staring at the taxi and its alighting passengers, but was too agitated to take any particular note of it, or them, when in a flash she saw her way of escape.

She was not thinking at all when she raced out of the hotel and bolted into the taxi. The cab driver seemed slightly surprised, but he appeared to have no objection to have another fare so soon. Panicking to be away,

Zarah gave him the only address in Oslo which came readily to mind.

Her wild panic began to ebb the nearer the taxi went to Fru Wenstad's apartment building. By the time the driver dropped her off at her destination, logic had returned, and Zarah was able to see what an utter idiot she had been to act so impetuously.

Of course Stein was not going to stay at the hotel! Where had her logic been that she could have thought he intended to stay in the same hotel—with a woman he had no liking for? Was it logical, when he cared so for his father, that he would leave the shaky, depressed man to cope on his own overnight!

Zarah shook away a mental picture of Stein turning round in the hotel to find her gone, and pressed the bell push to flat 2A. All she could think of was the interview before her, and Stein was forgotten.

Again she rang the bell, but again there was no answer. She made an abstracted half-turn, and was then shatteringly made to think of Stein. For—there he was! While she had been so churned up with her inner feelings that at any moment she would be face to face with Fru Wenstad, and had been oblivious to all sound, Stein's car had purred up to a halt not ten yards away!

Shaken rigid to see him standing beside his car watching her, Zarah felt panic again. This time, though, when she feared that he might know whom she was there to see, she managed to hold her panic down. Quickly her mind went into top gear, and she realised that since there was no name strip to indicate who lived at flat 2A, even if Stein came over to take a look, he would be none the wiser.

Unquestionably, though, her attempts to see Fru Wenstad were over for a while. Which left Zarah with nothing to do but to turn round and, if that grim look on Stein's face was anything to go by, face the music.

She adopted a cool air as she moved towards him. Her insides might feel wobbly, but he was never going to know that.

'We can't go on meeting like this,' she offered, as airily as possible.

He was not amused. Zarah halted when she was close enough to see from the steel in his eyes that he was not impressed by her show of bravado either. What he was, she could tell from the jut of his jaw, was all aggression. She had a very good idea that any moment now she was going to hear, hot and strong, what he thought of a woman who allowed him to fill in hotel registration documents on her behalf—and then bolted.

But she was proved wrong, for he did no such thing. What he did do, however, was to figuratively knock the legs from under her when, his tone as grim as his look, he said curtly:

'Had you asked, I could have told you that Gyda Wenstad moved from Oslo three months ago.' And, having all but floored her, his angry expression letting her know he'd had his fill of chasing around after her, 'Now,' he added grittily, 'run where the hell you like— I'm going back to Dalvik.'

CHAPTER EIGHT

STEIN was in his car when Zarah suddenly realised that her journey to Oslo was nothing but a wild goose chase. He had started up the car when she saw that to spend another minute in the capital would get her no further forward.

Suddenly she knew that she, like her aunt, had been seduced by Dalvik. Pulled by a need to be back in that beautiful place, she went swiftly to the driver's window.

Stein had noticed her, she knew, but when he did not look at her, she had an awful feeling he was just going to ignore her and drive off. When he did move to lower the window, she quickly forgot her pride, lest the window should suddenly start to go up again.

'Are you too mad at me to give me a lift home?' she ventured.

Her pride reared again when all Stein did was to survey her in stony silence. Certain he was about to make some withering comment about her 'home' being back in England, she took a step back on to the pavement.

Before her bridling anger led her to tell him what he could do with his lift, though, Stein spoke. And, uninviting though his words were, when he said, 'Get in,' and finalised the issue by closing the window, Zarah hesitated for only a moment, then went and 'got into' the passenger seat.

With Stein angry, and Zarah pricked by guilt that he had a right, she supposed, to be angry, it was in silence that they covered the first part of the journey. But as soon as she had decided, however, that the journey the rest of

120

the way would be covered in equal silence, suddenly, to her embarrassment, her stomach rumbled noisily. She looked out of the side window, aware when her stomach rumbled again that it was impossible for Stein not to have heard it.

'Have you eaten at all today?' he asked shortly when her stomach protested for a third time.

'I can't remember,' she lied just as shortly—then discovered that Stein was a man of instant decisions when he swung off the road they were travelling on and drew up outside a restaurant.

Her protests that she could wait for something to eat until they reached Dalvik were ignored. Her suggestion that he must want to get back to his father was treated likewise. In no time they were both sitting with plates of elk steaks and vegetables in front of them.

'You were hungry too, I see.' Zarah, fed up with being the one in the wrong, relieved herself of being the sole reason for the break in their journey.

'Why,' Stein delayed no longer to ask a question which she guessed all along he would at some time want answered, 'is it of importance for you to see Gyda Wenstad?'

She gave an offhand shrug. 'It isn't so important,' she lied. From his stern expression she saw that her answer was not good enough, and that he was waiting for more. She did not want to tell him more. Indeed, she had no intention of saying more. Yet somehow his very silence, his waiting silence, was forceful, so that in the end she just had to add, 'I just—wanted to see her.'

His short, 'The reason?' told her that he was not going to let up.

Strangely, at that point, she found that she hated lying to him. 'If you must know,' she snapped, irritated with herself, irritated with him, 'I . . . it was just that I felt I should like to talk to someone who had been my aunt's friend. Aunt Anne only occasionaly popped up in the conversations I had with my mother,' she explained cautiously, aware that with Stein being so astute she must not say too much. 'B-but with my mother dead, and Aunt Anne dead—and leaving me those shares—I realised I didn't know so very much about my aunt.'

She had told him as much as she was going to. Secretly she hoped that by inserting that thorn-in-the-side bit about the shares, she might have put paid to any further discussion.

It had not. Oddly, though, it was not the subject of shares, or her aunt, which Stein took up. But, considering he had previously scoffed at her stated desire to learn more of her aunt, this time he let it go.

'Have you no other relatives?' he questioned.

Blinking to know where the conversation was going now, 'No,' Zarah had to admit.

She was left staring. Because several moments after hearing her own that she had no other family, Stein, with no let-up in his hostility, was asking:

'Was I wrong? Did you come here, not in direct response to Langaard's letter, but because, when your mother died, you felt all alone in the world?'

Amazement struck her dumb. That Stein, who from the very first had believed nothing but the worst of her, should suddenly seem prepared to give her the benefit of the doubt, staggered her.

Confusion mixed in with her sudden aversion to tell him lies. 'No,' she replied honestly, too bemused to think to repeat that she had never received a letter from Olav Langaard. She then realised that she could run into trouble if she told Stein that, although she had felt lost when her mother died, her loneliness was not her prime motive in coming to Norway. Which left her with no option but to lie to him. 'I told you why I came,' she mumbled. 'The cottage I lived in belonged half to my aunt and . . .'

The glint that came to his eyes made her break off. He did not believe that tale now, any more than he had before, that much was plain. As was plain that he cared not at all to be lied to.

'So you arrive in Dalvik,' he documented tersely. 'You, belatedly,' he inserted sarcastically, 'find a need to know more about your aunt. But,' he went on sharply, 'when it would have been far more courteous to my father to ask him, or me, you opt to ask strangers for details of Anne's friends.'

One thing became very clear to Zarah. Stein had known, from the moment he had seen her at Fru Wenstad's old address, that she had gone outside the family to obtain that address—incorrect though that address was. Unable to confide the reason why she needed to see Fru Wenstad, even while she flinched from being branded a discourteous guest, Zarah had no other alternative but to come out fighting.

'I'm likely to ask you anything, aren't I?' she jeered, and worked up a head of steam to ignore the fact that but a moment ago there had seemed a possibility that he was giving her the benefit of the doubt. 'All I've ever got from you since I arrived has been to be labelled with one vile name after another!' Stein looked ready to shoot her down in flames, but she raged on heedlessly. 'As for asking your father . . .' Suddenly a picture of his father, defeated, worn with grief, was there in her head, and her fury, as quickly as it had erupted, fizzled out.

'My father?' Stein challenged toughly, daring her to say a word against his parent. 'What about him?'

'How could I ask him anything?' Zarah forced herself to snap. But she could not keep it up; Haldor had a warm place in her heart. 'He's hurting inside,' she said, her voice softer than it had been, 'I'd have to be as insensitive as the devil not to have seen that.'

Her sensitivity to his father left Stein unmoved as he showed he was not yet ready to leave the subject he had opened up. 'Having excluded both my father and me from your enquiries, you thought you could happily bandy your aunt's name abroad?'

'It wasn't like that!' she protested.

'You approached Fjeld,' he rapped bluntly.

'I didn't approach him!' Zarah was quick to disclaim, and would have clammed up, only Stein's scepticism, his obvious disbelief, made her go on to tell him as much as she dared. 'I asked him for directions—that day I went to the cemetery,' she told him begrudgingly. 'We—just— sort of got talking. He introduced himself, and I told him who I was. From there he said his mother and Fru Wenstad—only he didn't know her name was Fru Wenstad—not until his sister Leikny told him . . .'

'Leikny Moreite's in this too!'

'No!' Zarah denied forcefully. 'And there's *nothing* to be "in",' she added crossly. 'Anyway, I must have given Rolv the idea that I'd like to know more about the lady whose name he could not remember, because—when Leikny told him Fru Wenstead's name—he rang and invited me out to dinner.'

What Stein was thinking she could not guess. She knew, however, that her revelations thus far had earned her no merit marks when, as forthright as usual, he questioned:

'Are you saying you dined with Fjeld purely for the information he could give you?'

Hearing it put like that, Zarah saw she was little deserving of merit. But she dredged up an uncaring pose to help her over any self-ashamed feeling. 'So pin another label on me,' she retorted smartly.

Her defiant attitude had small effect, she noticed, for Stein was still not letting up. 'Do I gather it was not until yesterday that he told you Gyda Wenstad lived in Oslo?' Zarah decided she was fed up with Stein's questions, and refused to answer. Then she found he had taken her silence for confirmation, and that, having seen her talking to Rolv yesterday, he had just slotted everything into place. 'My God,' he said grimly, 'he had you eating out of his hand when he mentioned he would be going to Oslo today—you leapt at the chance to go with him!'

She had known in advance that Rolv was committed to go to Oslo today, but she refrained from telling Stein so, and instead she questioned insolently, 'How did you get to be so smart?'

'Where was your intelligence when you agreed to go with him?' he lobbed back at her. 'Or,' he questioned, his eyes as alert as ever, 'was your wish to meet Gyda Wenstad so important that you were prepared to do anything? Even,' he added, his tone hardening, 'if it meant risking your virginity?'

Zarah was instantly wary. Stein was as smart as she had dubbed him, and was too close. She had to do something, and fast, to prevent him from getting any closer.

'My—virginity—was never at risk,' she told him as evenly as she could. 'There's an essential goodness in Rolv which it doesn't take *too* much intelligence to spot,' she added with a weak stab at sarcasm. 'Nor,' she went on, noting that Stein did not appear thrilled to have Rolv's better qualities pointed out, 'was it so very important that I see Fru Wenstad.'

'You surprise me,' Stein offered his own brand of sarcasm.

'I should have explained more fully, only with you and me—er—not exactly the best of friends . . .' She left that bit there, to go on, 'Perhaps I might, in other circumstances, have told you of the delight I find in the beautiful scenery of your country.' Well, that at least was not a lie. 'Anyhow,' she continued, 'you'll have to agree that I've hardly been anywhere since I arrived.' That too was the truth.

'Apart from dinner with Fjeld, and a visit to see Langaard, you haven't set foot outside Dalvik until today,' he agreed.

'I'm not complaining, honestly I'm not,' Zarah told him, again truthfully. 'But when Rolv offered me the chance of a lift to Oslo, I thought it too good an opportunity to miss. To accept meant I could take in more scenery, take in Oslo—weather permitting,' she threw in a smile, 'and at the same time, I could perhaps call and have a chat with someone who had once been a friend of my aunt.'

Hoping she had not perjured her soul too much, Zarah did not know what else she could do to disabuse Stein of the idea that to see Fru Wenstad was of prime importance. She felt tense as she waited for him to make some reply. That tension, though, was to give way to relief when he did not return to the subject, but to her surprise, he informed her:

'As well as being a one-time friend with whom she kept in touch, Gyda Wenstad was highly valued by Anne for her skill with a sewing needle.'

'She sewed for my aunt?'

'Anne thought her work exquisite,' Stein nodded, and unbent sufficiently to outline how latterly, when any of his visits to Anne and his father would precede a business appointment in Oslo, he would sometimes drop off a parcel of material at Gyda Wenstad's apartment on Anne's behalf.

Zarah did her best to keep her expression no more than interested, but the thought that maybe the trail to find Fru Wenstad was not ended was at the forefront of her mind. Into her head shot a memory of Stein saying that Fru Wenstad had left Oslo three months ago. Could it be that, since she had moved, he had dropped off another parcel for Anne? Did he, in fact, know where Fru Wenstad lived now?

How she held back from asking him then and there if he knew Fru Wenstad's new address, Zarah could not have said. But, having sweated to convince him that for her to see the seamstress was not of paramount importance, she knew that all her efforts would be wasted if she did ask. She decided, rather than to push her luck, that she had better let the smoke clear first. Perhaps tomorrow she might, casually, make the enquiry.

'I've eaten all I need,' she took the conversation into a totally different sphere.

Stein gave her a shrewd scrutiny, and Zarah smiled. He did not smile, and unsmiling, he escorted her from the restaurant.

The remainder of their journey was completed without either of them saying very much. With a brief, 'Good night,' Zarah left Stein to garage the car, and went into the house and up to her room.

Strangely, her waking feeling the next morning was one of happiness with an inner contentment to be back in Dalvik. The feeling did not last. No sooner did she start to relive that time of tension, deceit, and discovery in that restaurant which Stein had pulled up at, than any small peace of mind she had found was wrecked. She had to find out Fru Wenstad's address, she just had to.

Suddenly, though, she experienced the most peculiar feeling of shyness at the thought of seeing Stein again. By the time she was ready to go downstairs, she had re-diagnosed that feeling. It wasn't shyness, it was just a fear that if she got her timing wrong, then she could very well let herself in for another third degree from him on the subject of her interest in Fru Wenstad.

The time, she saw as soon as she joined Stein and his father for breakfast, was definitely not right. For although Stein answered her 'Good morning,' civilly enough, he had nothing more to say to her.

She knew sufficient of him by then to know that to get him on his own and then to plough in straight away with the sixty-four-dollar question would make him too suspicious.

She had just consigned herself to patience, and was resigned that she would just have to bide her time, when all at once Haldor, who had been his usual faraway self, suddenly surprised her by saying:

'You're here! I thought you were in Oslo?'

Zarah sent him a smile, but with no wish to confuse him further than he was confused already, she kept it brief as she told him, 'Stein gave me a lift back.'

'Stein!' he exclaimed, and Zarah saw that confused was an understatement, for he seemed to have no recollection that it was he who had asked his son to come to Oslo after her.

'It was pouring with rain when Stein spotted me sitting in a restaurant,' she explained carefully. 'He joined me on an organised sightseeing tour, then . . .' she drew a thick veil over the way she had left Stein checking her in at a hotel, and ended simply, '. . . then we came home.'

She rather guessed it was the way she had called his home *her* home that was responsible for Haldor's reaction. For as his glance went quickly from her and to his son, and then back again to her, suddenly a beam of delight started to break on his face—and Haldor was very definitely smiling.

The next moment, though, as if to stress that if his father was delighted that she thought of the Norwegian home as her home then he most positively was not, Stein had butted in abruptly to change the conversation.

'Herr Juvkam was well when you saw him yesterday?' he asked his parent.

'Extremely,' Haldor replied, his expression thoughtful. 'I have agreed to sell him the boat,' he remembered.

Monday gave way to Tuesday, and Tuesday gave way to Wednesday, with Stein in Zarah's opinion growing more and more unapproachable with the passing of each day. She had many times rehearsed some innocent-sounding way of putting her question, but by Thursday—again taking over on the housekeeper's day off—that question had still not been put.

When Zarah awoke on Friday, she knew that today was the day. Her patience to wait for the right moment had run out.

She had to be patient for a while longer, however. Because, throughout that day, whenever she acted on a moment of courage to go and seek Stein out, he just never seemed to be around. Had he been deliberately trying to avoid her, she fretted, he could not have been more successful. Consequently, when the time drew near for the evening meal and she had still not had her private word with him, Zarah determined, whether she had the courage or not, that she was going to buttonhole him immediately dinner was over.

She had worked herself up into a fine state of inner turmoil when twenty minutes later she sat down to dinner. Just how was she to ask to see Stein privately, and then ask him for Fru Wenstad's address as though it was immaterial whether he gave it to her or not?

She was still nursing her dilemma when Haldor who, although he had raised his eyes to glance occasionally at her and sometimes at Stein, suddenly had something to say. What he said—bearing in mind that seldom, in his depressed state, did he go anywhere without Stein by his side—had the effect of a minor bombshell.

'I have decided,' he began, when he had done little in the way of decision-making just lately apart from deciding to sell his boat, 'to go fishing this weekend.'

Instantly Zarah forgot her own problems. If she felt concern for Haldor, though, she knew that it was with a mixture of pleasure and concern that Stein had heard his father take what might be a giant step towards recapturing the threads of his life.

'You—want to go fishing?' he asked.

'You would prefer I stayed at home?' Haldor questioned, his expression, which was more normally tired and worn, appearing to Zarah to be strangely innocent.

'Of course not, *Far*,' Stein denied, and showed how much he approved of the idea by adding, 'It's too late to get off tonight, but we can . . .'

Haldor clearing his throat, and stating, 'Umph—hmm . . . I'm going with Brage Juvkam,' made Stein break off. Whereupon Haldor explained how his friend Brage had told him last Sunday that he intended to spend a few weeks at his summer cabin commencing this Saturday, and how he had invited him along. 'I telephoned him this afternoon,' Haldor ended as he neatly folded his serviette, 'to say I had decided to accept.'

It took Stein no time to digest what his father had just said, and his voice had a pleased ring to it when, apparently knowing the location of Brage Juvkam's summer cabin, he stated, 'It's a fair distance, we'd better get off early.'

Haldor had risen and was ready to leave the dining room when, his look full of the high regard with which he held his son, he told him, 'There's no need for you to drive me there.'

'You're going to drive yourself?' To Zarah's ears, Stein sounded not at all sure that he liked the idea.

Haldor shook his head. 'My—concentration—is not quite what it should be,' he confessed. 'But Brage has said he will call for me on his way. I'd be glad, though,' he added, and seemed to visibly brighten, 'if you could come and pick me up some time on Sunday.'

'Any time you say,' Stein agreed willingly. He too was on his feet when Haldor, about to go through the door, stayed long enough to embarrass Zarah to death.

'It will mean a long drive for you, Stein,' he said. 'Perhaps Zarah will come with you for company.'

He had gone before she could invent a dozen and one things which would keep her busy on Sunday. She hesitated to look at Stein, because she didn't need two guesses to know that he would by far prefer his own company than to have to share hers.

When she did flick a glance at him, though, she saw from his thoughtful expression that his anxieties over his father must weigh heavily with him. Her embarrassment swiftly disappeared, as she gave in to the impulse of the moment.

'He'll be all right, Stein,' she just had to say. 'Try not to worry . . .' Some of her impulsiveness took a dive when cool grey eyes flicked down to where she was seated, but, nothing if not game, she made herself go on. 'It could be that a fishing trip might be of a help in this time of him trying to come to terms with his grief.'

There followed a taut silence when, if anything, she fully expected to be told to keep her nose out of something which was not her business; then that silence was broken, 'I think,' said Stein, 'that he has started to come to terms with losing his dear Anne. I think,' he went on to astonish her after another moment of silent thought, 'that you, Zarah, have been a help to him in these dark days of his grief.'

'*Me!*' she exclaimed, astounded as much by what he had said, as she was that it was *he* who had said it. 'Good heavens,' she said faintly, quite well aware of the way Stein daily watched over his father, 'I've done nothing!'

She was more thunderstruck than ever when grey eyes which had but a moment ago seemed cool took on a warm look. Stein even smiled as he replied:

'So you may believe. But I've noticed a definite change for the better in my father since you've been here.' Stunned again, Zarah dragged her eyes from his mouth, and was about to tell Stein that any change for the better in Haldor had to be no more than a natural day-to-day progression—for when one had hit rock bottom, the only way was up. But suddenly Stein had sent any thought of saying such words flying, and her anger was spontaneous when he followed up his previous remark with a considered, 'Which makes me think I owe you some reward.'

Up in arms in a split second, Zarah was on her feet. 'Don't you *dare* offer me money!' she flared, her sleeves immediately rolled up for a pitched battle, for Stein had never hidden behind the door when it came to firing straight from the shoulder. But, to cause her no little confusion, he did not fire an angry return, but, his look mild, he said quietly:

'I wasn't going to.'

'You—weren't?' she questioned warily.

Again Stein smiled. 'I merely thought it might please you if I took you to see Gyda Wenstad tomorrow.'

To say Zarah was flabbergasted did not begin to cover

it. All this week she had been building herself up to ask him if he knew Fru Wenstad's address, and now, without her even having to ask, Stein was telling her that not only did he know her address, but that he would take her there—it was incredible! But an opposing instinct to the one that wanted to snatch at his offer with both hands warned her that she must not show herself to be too eager. Stein must not know how important it was to her.

'Does she live far away?' she asked.

'She and her husband live on the outskirts of Fagernes. We can make it there and back in a day.'

'I—should quite like to chat with her,' Zarah accepted carefully, and saw that as far as Stein was concerned, the matter was settled.

'We'll get off as soon as my father and Herr Juvkam have gone,' he told her.

There seemed nothing more to say. Zarah made for the door. 'I'll be ready,' she said, and went to bed.

Her sleep was fitful. Mixed in with her anxiety about what she might learn from Fru Wenstad tomorrow were confused thoughts about Stein. That he would be beholden to no one was clear. That he wanted no outstanding debt for the improvement he had seen in his father was also clear. Whether she had convinced him that to see Fru Wenstad was not of paramount importance, or whether she hadn't, Stein quite plainly, in his search to settle his debt, had never forgotten her one-time wish to see that lady. Which, since he had not offered her some material reward, made Zarah wonder—while experiencing the most unexpected fluttering in her heart region—had he changed his low opinion of her?

Brage Juvkam, a man about the same age as Haldor Kildedalen, arrived just after breakfast the following morning. Haldor introduced him to Zarah, and after a few pleasantries, the two men were about to make tracks for the summer cabin, when Brage Juvkam suddenly exclaimed something in Norwegian, then dipped his hand into his jacket pocket.

Lost to what was going on, Zarah stood by while he extracted a bulky envelope and, with another comment in his own tongue, passed the envelope over to Haldor. Whereupon Haldor, who always insisted on speaking English while she was there, replied in Norwegian and, turning to hand the envelope to Stein, was reminded of Zarah standing beside his son. 'My friend here,' Haldor remarked, 'who shuns the use of a chequebook, almost forgot his special visit to the bank yesterday.'

None the wiser as to what was going on, Zarah heard Stein say that he would put the envelope in the safe, but it seemed to take another fifteen minutes before they eventually waved the two men off. Then Stein was saying pleasantly, 'Shall we go too?'

'I'll just get my bag.'

Zarah left him to go upstairs where she was suddenly so beset by nerves about her impending talk with Fru Wenstad that she would not have been upset had Stein called the visit off.

She dallied in her room for far longer than it should have taken her to collect her bag. But Stein did not comment on it when she joined him in the hall.

When other journeys with him had for the most part been silent, though, it was when they later stopped for lunch that he did comment, 'You're very quiet this morning.'

'Who wouldn't be?' she said, forcing a smile. 'My breath's taken away at the scenery.'

She turned her attention to her meal, but, with her stomach knotted up, she was able to get very little down. Not wishing for Stein to remark on that too, she searched her mind for some topic of conversation. But with the whole of her attention centred on the forthcoming meeting, the only thing to come into her head was something she had not previously paused to consider.

'I've just thought . . .' she said quickly, '. . . what if Fru Wenstad isn't in when we get there?'

'She will be,' Stein replied, his confidence amazing her, until he added, 'I telephoned her last night.'

'Oh!' Zarah exclaimed, and made what was a tremendous effort, to say lightly, 'now why didn't I think of doing that?'

'Probably,' said Stein, a quirk appearing at the corners of his mouth, 'because you don't know her phone number.'

Zarah knew then that her inner tumult was getting the better of her. Because whether or not Stein had intended her to be amused by his reply, amused was what she was. She laughed.

The break in her tension was brief, however. When in the early afternoon Stein pulled up at a hillside house, she was tenser than ever.

Gyda Wenstad proved to be a warm and motherly woman. 'Come in, come in,' she beamed once the introductions were over, and would have turned to lead the way had not Stein moved a step back, and excused himself.

'I see Egil's in his garage. I'll go and have a word.'

In her tense state, Zarah felt nothing but gratitude to Stein. Had he sat with her throughout he entire visit, their trip might just as well not have been made. For there was no way she could have asked what she needed to ask while he was there.

She followed Gyda Wenstad indoors, and knew an urgency to have her conversation out of the way—Stein might come in at any moment. That urgent feeling made her refuse the offer of refreshment. 'We had lunch only a short while ago,' she stretched the truth a little. Then she found that the gods were on her side when, saying she would make some tea when Stein and her husband came in, her hostess tendered her condolences, which took the conversation straight to Anne, and added:

'It is such pleasantness to meet you, Miss Thornton.'

'Please call me Zarah,' she smiled, wondering if it was too soon to introduce the subject, not of first names, but of surnames.

'You resemble Anne when you smile,' Gyda Wenstad observed, and the moment to introduce the subject was lost.

'You've known—knew—her for a very long time, I believe?'

'Almost from when she left England,' the motherly woman agreed, and as Zarah's palms started to grow moist in case Stein might come in at any moment, she could delay no longer.

'My aunt would have been known as Miss Gentry, in those days?' she questioned, ready to grab at any opening. She had built herself up for this moment, but as Zarah waited for a reply, she was so tense she was hardly breathing. It was therefore a gigantic anti-climax when, after a moment or two of casting her mind back, Fru Wenstad shook her head.

'Was that Anne's name? It is so long ago,' she smiled. 'I cannot recall knowing her by any name but Anne Kildedalen.' She smiled again as she confided, 'With Herr Kildedalen so in love with her, it was not a long time before he changed her name to his.'

Zarah made mammoth efforts to hide her feelings, but because some comment was needed, she asked what she already knew, 'Uncle Haldor—he was very much in love with Anne?'

'I have never seen a love like it,' Gyda Wenstad

answered softly. 'He worshipped her, and could not bear her out of his sight. But,' her warm smile came out again, 'if he was possessive of her, Anne was happy he was so.'

'She loved him as he loved her?' Zarah asked, when just then her keen ears picked up the sound of movement from outside.

She only half heard her hostess's warmly confirming, 'Oh yes!' The desperate notion had just occurred to her that perhaps Egil Wenstad would remember by what name Anne had been known.

With no time to delay, 'Your husband would remember my aunt in those early days too?' she asked.

Her last remaining hope was scuttled when Fru Wenstad shook her head. 'Egil was at sea for the first years of our marriage,' she explained. 'Only later, when Anne would visit Oslo and call to see me, did he meet her. He . . .' She broke off as the door opened and her husband and Stein came in.

The topic was dropped when Stein introduced Zarah to Egil Wenstad, and Egil's wife went to make some refreshment. The next hour got under way, with Stein, as if conscious that Zarah had not had much time for a chat about her aunt, leading the conversation into that quarter.

When they made leaving noises, Zarah had heard enough to know that, whatever else had gone on in Anne's life, she had been sublimely happy with Haldor.

Zarah did not know if she was disappointed or what she was on that return journey to Dalvik. Having steeled herself to go through with the visit to Fru Wenstad, having beaten back cowardice to face whatever there was to face, she knew only that she now felt emotionally drained and flattened.

She was staring unseeing through the windscreen, and contemplating the fact that she had learned nothing, when Stein's voice suddenly penetrated her thoughts.

'You seem—upset, Zarah. Did you not hear for yourself that Anne was happy with my father?' he asked.

Only then did she become aware that they had been motoring for an age, and not one solitary word had left her. 'Yes,' she roused herself to answer, 'I heard that.'

'You sound as though you don't believe it,' he said evenly, but the edge that lurked in his tone told her that he had taken exception to her quiet reply.

'I believe it,' she said, but did not miss his quick look of realisation that, for once, she was not rolling up her sleeves to meet any aggression from him head-on.

Too defeated just then to want to do battle with him or anyone else, she was uncaring of the tautness of his expression. She had other matters on her mind.

Again and again she sifted through every word that had been said—but that took her not the smallest step forward. Anne had been happy with Haldor. Haldor had been happy with Anne. He had been possessive of her— hadn't Rolv Fjeld said something of the same sort too— in any event, Anne had obviously liked it that way.

They stopped at a restaurant an hour or so later when Stein told her that he had given Fru Onsvag the day off, and that they would have an early dinner. But again Zarah had no appetite. She observed that he was looking more granite faced than ever as they left the restaurant, but her spirits had sunk so low, it hardly mattered to her how he looked.

She tried to resign herself to the fact that she was never going to know for sure which sister had given her birth, and as they reached Dalvik, she even argued, what good would it do to know anyway? But, by the time Stein had pulled up outside the house, the only thing she was resigned to was that it was just going to have to niggle away at her for ever. Because, unless she wanted to risk stirring up a whole hornets' nest, there was no one else she could ask.

For once Stein did not bother to garage the car, and he was right there with her when she went into the house. Nor, she discovered, was he in a very amiable frame of mind. For when she would have left him and gone up to her room, he caught hold of her arm, detained her, and turned her about. Sombrely she eyed him as, without preamble, he charged:

'Today's visit doesn't appear to have given you any pleasure.'

Belatedly, she realised that she had been most tardy with her thanks. Stein had put himself out for her today, and must, she thought, be taking her to task for her lack of manners.

'Thank you for taking me to see Fru Wenstad,' she said politely, but brushing her words aside, he demanded:

'What's wrong?'

Alarm started to spear her when she realised from his expression that he seemed determined to get to the bottom of what was upsetting her.

'Nothing's wrong,' she mumbled, and made for the stairs—only she had forgotten that he still had hold of her arm.

'I'm not buying that!' He swung her back to face him. His expression was aggression-filled, she saw, but nowhere could she find the fire she needed with which to meet it.

'Leave me alone,' she said, desperate to get away. Because, suddenly, she felt the stirrings of an urge to confide in him.

'Not until you tell me what it is that troubles you,' Stein insisted. 'You've said barely a word all day—you've eaten nothing. You've . . .'

'I'm not hungry,' Zarah interrupted, and knew only

then, as that urge to confide became a compelling urge, that she had to escape, or give in. Wildly she jerked out of his grip and raced for her room.

Unfortunately, fast though she went, Stein went with her. When she entered her room Stein entered too. But where she was a mass of agitation, he was calm.

Calmly it was that he closed the door—and cut off any other attempt at escape. And he was calm too when, looking into her panicking brown eyes, he said:

'You have today discovered how happy Anne was in her life here. I,' he said firmly, 'mean to discover, before this day is over, what it is that is making you so unhappy.'

CHAPTER NINE

DESPERATE for some of his calm, Zarah knew she had made a mistake to fly to her room. She should have known better. Stein in determined mood was not a man to let anyone run.

'I'm not unhappy,' she denied.

'Don't lie to me,' he retorted. 'I know something's troubling you.'

'I'm not lying,' she argued, wishing he would leave her alone. 'There's nothing troubling me. Y-you're imagining it.'

'Am I?' he said toughly. 'Have I imagined you sad beside me all the way back? Have I imagined a defeated spirit in you?' he scorned. 'Had I not known you, had I not had first-hand experience of the way you fly at me on the smallest provocation, I might be taken in. But . . .'

'Smallest provocation!' Zarah was sufficiently side-tracked to exclaim, but there was no heat in her words either.

'But,' he continued shortly as if she had not spoken, 'when, until today, I have known nothing but spirited response from you—no matter how unpleasant . . .'

'Unpleasant?' she interrupted, in an endeavour to deflect him from his purpose. She then wished he had ignored her second utterance, as he had ignored her first, because suddenly he had stilled, and with his eyes fixed firmly on her, he was qualifying:

'Perhaps not always unpleasant. There was a—pleasant—response from you once.' Suddenly she knew what he was going to say, and as for no reason her heart

141

began to race, she wanted to halt him. But it was too late for that. Even as she opened her mouth, Stein was recalling, 'I kissed you, and you . . .'

'Don't remind me,' she cut him off, and immediately saw her mistake when a muscle jerked in his temple and as if he was the one who was tension-filled, and not her, he moved forward and asked quietly:

'You are trying to forget that kiss, Zarah?'

A gamut of emotions was all at once let loose inside her, and feeling backed into a corner, Zarah could take no more. 'If you won't leave my room,' she said coldly, 'then I will.' With that, she moved towards and round him. She had her hand on the door handle, when Stein moved.

Her back was to him when, by placing a hand on either of her arms, he stopped her from leaving. Her pulses started to pound, and she knew herself vulnerable to his touch. The tingling sensation his fingers on her arms aroused defeated all her efforts to summon up some aggression, so that her voice was husky as she said, 'Let me go, Stein.'

Any lingering hope of finding that aggression she so badly needed was scattered to the four winds. Had he remained stern, harsh, or just cool, she thought she might have managed it. But Stein was gentle, and the never-before-heard gentleness in his voice was just too much.

'Share with me, sweet Zarah,' he said softly into her ear. 'Tell me what troubles you.'

A trembling started somewhere inside her as she heard Stein call her sweet Zarah. And the weakness that assaulted her threatened to have her cave in when he moved her so that the back of her head rested against his broad manly chest.

'I—can't,' she moaned, and knew even as she gave in to a need for solace, and leant her head against him, that she could not and must not tell him.

'Trust me,' he breathed, and gently turned her, his arms coming about her. Zarah saw warmth emanating from the grey eyes that fastened on to her. That warmth was almost her undoing. 'Trust me, Zarah,' he urged. 'Tell me!'

'Oh, Stein!' left her in anguish, and she was concentrating so hard on keeping a close guard on her tongue that it left her physical being totally unprotected. When Stein, as if he too was suddenly without protection, began to lower his head, Zarah was defenceless.

Their lips met, and that same gentleness she had seen and heard was there in Stein's kiss. Peace washed over her. She wanted more. Stein raised his head, and seeing the warmth his eyes still held, Zarah could offer no resistance when his lips returned to hers.

A feeling of joy flooded her when, holding her close to his heart, he deepened his kiss. She felt the strength of him as his arms tightened about her, and yet, although he had the strength to crush her bruisingly, his hold retained a touch of gentleness.

His lips were at her throat, and she heard him murmur something in Norwegian. She did not know what he said, but the husky quality of his voice was a caress. Her arms wound around him, and passion soared when, gently, he began to ignite a fire in her.

Kiss for kiss she gave him. When minutes later he gentled her towards the bed, she was so consumed with a need for him, she went willingly to lie with him and to marvel that he was capable of such tenderness.

Stein kissed her eyes, her ears, and trailed kisses down her throat. She felt his hands warm at the fastenings of her clothing, and gloried at the feel of his kiss on her naked shoulders.

His hands caressed her back, pulling her to him, and she pressed to get nearer still. A groan left him, and she heard him breathe a shaken, 'Do you know what you're doing to me?' but she was too lost in his kisses to reply.

She had long since forgotten how this had all started, and had no thought in her head as to where it was leading. All she knew was that Stein had started an inferno in her, and as his hand caressed her breast, she knew that she wanted to explore with him wherever he led—or so she thought.

Enthralled by him, enraptured to be in his arms, she had no room in her head for anything or anyone but him. But suddenly, as that hand caressed from her breast to her waist and down to the inside of her skirt, so while most of her felt only joy at his touch, she was visited by a deeply hidden dart of inhibition.

'No!' jerked from her. Immediately, Stein removed his hand. Immediately, Zarah wanted him to put it back again. She almost told him so, but, too swift in his efforts to soothe, Stein had spoken first.

'It's all right,' he said gently. 'You have nothing to fear, *min kjaereste*.'

Stunned, she felt her heart take a wild leap. *Kjaereste* was Norwegian for 'darling', she was sure it was. The realisation that Stein had just called her his darling held her dumb. The wonder of the truth that had just come to her—that she was in love with him—had her staring at him, and unable to speak. Stein moved a hand to cup one side of her face when, perhaps taking her muteness for disquiet at this new territory he had taken her to, he again gentled her.

'Trust me, *elskling*,' he murmured. 'Trust me.'

Ready to trust him, more than willing to give him her trust, at that precise moment, to shatter her completely, her memory awoke to remind her that she had heard him speak those same two words, 'Trust me', not so long ago. Pain streaked through her. Oh God, she thought, and felt quite ill.

Her emotions in an uproar, frantically Zarah pushed Stein from her and scrambled off the bed. With agitated fingers she did what she could to get her clothing into some sort of order. But the whole time she was beating back a feeling of hysteria at the knowledge that Stein had only made love to her so that, in pillow talk, he might get from her what she would not tell him any other way.

'There's nothing to panic over, little Zarah.' Stein had left the bed to come and stand near her. 'Did I not stop the moment our lovemaking became too—intimate—for you to handle in one leap from your novice state?' he asked, still in that same soothing tone.

'You might have stopped, briefly,' Zarah fired, all the aggression she had wanted there in that moment as her emotions teetered on the edge. 'But if I hadn't . . . if . . . You'd have had another attempt at seducing me if I hadn't . . .'

'Seducing you!' Stein sounded astonished. His soothing tone had soon disappeared, she noticed, when, his tone more like a roar, he blasted, 'Damn you—it was mutual!'

'Like hell it was!' she yelled. 'You deliberately set out to seduce me!' she accused.

She gave him full marks that, in the face of her being emotionally out of gear, he pretended to try to see what had happened from her point of view. For he controlled the fury her accusation had brought, and quietly he tried to reason:

'I know you have no previous experience in . . .'

'I'm not applying for a job!' Zarah cut in angrily.

'You misunderstand . . .'

'Like hell I misunderstand!' she blazed. 'Why, you're

no better than Rolv Fjeld. Worse, in fact,' she erupted. 'At least with him I had a glimmering of what might have been in his mind when I went away with him.'

'What, exactly,' Stein enquired icily, his attempt to reason with her shortlived in the face of being compared to Rolv Fjeld, 'are you saying?'

'I'm saying,' Zarah, in full throttle, did not hold back from throwing at him, 'that I'd much sooner have a man I *know* I can't trust than a man who implores me to do just that.' She ignored the arrogant look that mingled with his icy expression, and charged on. 'A man who's so piqued at not having my trust that, if he has to, he's quite prepared to seduce me to get it!'

Stein's voice was arctic. 'Have you quite finished?' he clipped.

'You want more?' scorned Zarah, and weathered his chilling look.

'You have said ample,' he said curtly, and strode to the door. But, as Zarah was feeling she would collapse if he did not soon go, he turned from the door and, his English curt and precise, he stayed to inform her cuttingly, 'Since it apears you have some slight interest in airing the truth, permit me to tell you—truthfully—that when it comes to seduction, until you decided you wanted to keep your precious virginity, I have seldom had a woman more willing.'

The long hours of the night seemed to go on for ever. Zarah tried hard to hate Stein when, with his pride-wounding parting shot, he had left her. But it was no good. She loved him, was in love with him. He had stormed her emotions from the beginning.

At four o'clock, in an effort to concentrate on something else, she went and took a bath, but Stein just refused to get out of her head.

Devil, him and his 'Trust me'! Why she should trust

him? she would like to know. 'You misunderstand', he had said. What was there to misunderstand, for goodness' sake! He had been piqued that she would not confide in him, and that was all there was to it. She had misunderstood nothing.

Nothing, she re-endorsed, as she stepped out of the bath and rubbed herself dry. Not unless Stein was sincere, had she misunderstood a ... Her thoughts suddenly halted, and all at once she was riveted to the spot. When had she ever known Stein to be anything but sincere? When had she ever known him back away from the truth?

Zarah left the bathroom and, seeing no point in going to bed, with her thoughts darting in all directions, she got dressed. Ten minutes later she had got herself sufficiently together for her thoughts to form some kind of a shape.

Her emotions had been all haywire when Stein had said 'Trust me' and she had shot from the bed. She had not been thinking at all then, she had to own. Which, bearing in mind what Stein had done to her senses, not to mention the realisation that she was in love with him, was hardly surprising.

Zarah pushed on, to try to see how things would have appeared to her if she had not been in such a highly charged emotional state. What if Stein had been sincere? What if she had truly misunderstood? Why, she questioned, would it be so important for Stein to want her trust? Why had he wanted to share whatever was troubling her?

Had he just been observing the courtesies to a guest in his father's house? Was it just from a feeling that she should be both mentally and physically comfortable that he had tried to get her to confide her troubles to him?

Remembering the way he had been with her until recently, she realised that Stein couldn't have cared less

about her mental and physical welfare. Those two words,
though, 'until recently', suddenly jumped back into her
head—and refused to leave.

Her thoughts flew to the time when Stein had brought
her back from Oslo. They had stopped for a meal and
she, she easily recalled, had been amazed that he might
be ready to revise what he thought of her, when he had
asked, 'Was I wrong?'

She remembered how, on Friday, she had flared up at
him when she had thought he was about to offer her
money. 'I wasn't going to,' he had answered, and Zarah
had lain awake that night wondering if he had changed
his low opinion of her.

If he had changed his low opinion, though, what had
made him revise his previously strongly held view of her?
Was it anything tangible at all? Suddenly, hearing again
Stein's sincere 'Trust me', his 'You misunderstand',
Zarah found herself in the realms of fantasy. Could it be
that Stein, like her, felt something which was the entire
opposite of—hate?

She could not believe it. And yet the idea, once born,
would not go away. Again and again she had to ask—was
there a chance that Stein felt something for her? Had she
been too hasty to accuse? Would Stein have explained
what she did not 'understand' had she given him the
chance?

It did not take her long to realise that she was never
going to have any misunderstanding cleared up—not
unless she, in turn, could confide freely in Stein.

Brought down to earth with a bump, Zarah knew she
could no more tell Stein today what was troubling her
than she could yesterday. Her uncertainty that he could
care anything for her made her shy away from giving him
that confidence. How could she tell him anything when
she still did not know if she was Margaret's daughter, or

the daughter of Anne? Aside from anything else, there was his father to consider. Haldor . . .

Suddenly, perhaps because she had thought for so long about Stein and in so doing had given her other problem a rest from continuous questioning, all at once Zarah started to see more light. New thoughts began to stir.

The whole of her torment had begun with a marriage certificate, but what about the marriage certificate of Anne and Haldor? Why, oh, why hadn't she thought before? All she had to do was to get in touch with the Norwegian records office, and her search would be at an end!

Talk about not being able to see the wood for the trees! There was she thinking she would never know, while the answer had been there the whole time! It would all be recorded—must be. The date, the place, and—the name which Anne had used when she had married Haldor. All she had to do was find the date the marriage had taken place and . . .

Her thoughts came to an abrupt halt. Who was she to ask for that marriage date? From the aloof look on Stein's face when he had left her room, she would be lucky if he ever spoke to her again. Haldor, then?

Zarah had to reject asking Haldor. By virtue of the fact that he had started to take a small interest in life by going fishing with Brage Juvkam, she had to decide it was better not to give him anything to dwell on with regard to Anne.

Impatiently, Zarah saw she could be in for months of backwards and forwards correspondence between herself and the records authorities if she could not furnish them with an accurate date.

The thought of having to wait more long months had her feeling frustrated before she had so much as written her first letter. But all at once, out of that frustrated feeling, something else suddenly hit her. Surely, somewhere in the house, there must be the original copy of that marriage certificate?

It was a little after five o'clock when, like a thief in the night, Zarah crept from her room and tiptoed down the stairs. She had waited long enough—she just could not wait any longer. Haldor would value that marriage certificate—she knew just where it would be.

On slippered feet, she went swiftly along the hall, and was blind and deaf to anything but that she was within an ace of her goal. Noiselessly she opened the study door and went in. In no time she had lifted down the box files that concealed the safe. She knew the combination.

A familiar sickness caught her stomach, and she had to halt for a moment before she could turn the dial in accordance with her aunt's birthday. Did she really want to know?

Thoughts of how she wanted to confide in Stein pushed her on. The safe opened easily once she had fed it the correct code, but her first sight of its contents showed that very little was kept there.

Methodically she went to work. First she took everything out from the safe and laid the various papers upside down on the desk. Then, in reverse order, she went through everything.

Within minutes Zarah knew she was going to have to take the long way round, and write to the records office. There was nothing remotely resembling a marriage certificate among those forms and documents.

Having built herself up to open the wretched safe in the first place, she was about to close it when she realised she would never make an industrial spy. For, careful to leave everything exactly as she had found it, she saw she had not put everything back.

The bulky envelope seemed destined to be forgotten,

she thought glumly, as she took it from the desk. It appeared to be the same envelope which Brage Juvkam had almost forgotten to give Haldor yesterday. Stein must have popped it into the safe before they had left to visit Fru . . .

A sudden sound in the silence made her break off midthought. Startled, she looked up to see that Stein, a fully dressed Stein, had walked into the study.

There was no thought in her head of how she must appear standing by the open safe with the bulky envelope in her hands. All she was aware of, in those initial tense seconds, was her love for him, and how, only hours ago, they had lain together in passionate embrace.

Warm colour flushed her cheeks at the memory of the lovemaking they had shared, and her inner emotion was such that it did not register that, in contrast, Stein's face had drained of colour.

That was until, while she stood rooted, he moved suddenly. Then she took in his white face and his savage expression. In a few furious strides he was up to her, but she was so shaken by his fierce expression that a jerky, 'I w-was looking for . . .' had escaped her before she realised that she could still not tell him anything.

'I can *see*—you found it!' Stein exploded thunderously.

'Found . . .' Zarah echoed blankly, and only then, as she followed the blaze of his glance at the package in her hands, did it dawn on her how it must look to him. As though it was a hot brick, she dropped the envelope to the desk. 'I . . .'

But he was too enraged to listen. 'By God, you need to look guilty!' he shouted, and, never more incensed, he grabbed up the envelope and tore it open. 'Here,' he snarled, 'take it!' So saying, he upended the envelope and thrust what must be the Norwegian equivalent of thousands of pounds at her.

'I don't want it!' she shrieked and tried to push the money back at him—which only incensed him the more.

'Was *I* fooled!' he bellowed. 'No wonder you were quiet yesterday! You had a lot to think about, didn't you?

'I . . .'

'The only thing that troubled you yesterday,' he rode straight over her attempt to get a word in, 'was how to get hold of the cash deposit you knew Herr Juvkam had paid for my father's boat, without bringing suspicion on yourself.'

Furious on the instant, Zarah was not prepared to let anybody accuse her of being a thief—no matter how redhanded she might appear to have been caught. 'How dare . . .' she erupted. But Stein was no nearer to letting her get a word in than he had been before.

'How long did it take you to work it out?' he raged.

'I didn't work anything . . .'

'With a brain like yours it shouldn't have taken all day,' he sliced through her denial, gave a grunt as something obviously just occurred to him, and then raged on, 'It wasn't until I told you I'd given Fru Onsvag the day off that you had it all mapped out. It was to be burglary—by another hand—while we were all out. Had I not come in and caught you, you'd have crept back to your room with the money, to be as appalled as the rest of us when the robbery was discovered.'

'*No!*' Zarah shouted. 'You're . . .

'Wasn't the wealth Anne left you enough?' he grated, his fury with her never letting up. 'What is it with you, that you had to get your greedy hands on some ready money now? Couldn't you wait—is that it?' he barked, his jaw jutting at a dangerous angle. 'You couldn't,' he decided. 'No matter what it would do to my father, no matter how it might set him back to believe that intruders had been through the house and violated articles which Anne had loved, you couldn't wait. You care only for yourself,' he reviled her, 'and care not a damn for him, for . . .'

Zarah's right hand, rocketing through the air, caught him a stinging blow to the side of his face. In the frustration of not being allowed to get a word in, her fury by then such that she could contain it no longer, she stopped Stein and relieved her anger in the only way left open to her.

She was suddenly afraid. Because before the sound of her furious slap had died away, Stein's rage had broken out of bounds. She saw his hand cut through the air, and in the split second of his intention being telegraphed, she braced herself to be knocked off her feet.

It never happened. How he managed to regain some self-control to cancel the blow before it could land, she couldn't tell. But suddenly, his face whiter than ever, he seemed to have come to the realisation that he had been within a few inches of hitting her, and both his hands were down at his sides. She heard the clench of his teeth, and as if uncertain he would not yet lay about her, in the next second he had turned about and abruptly left the room.

Shattered by what had taken place, Zarah could not move for several minutes. Then, as if some automaton was in charge, she collected up the scattered money. Neatly she placed it inside the envelope. Tidily she placed it inside the safe. Methodically she closed the safe and returned the box files to their correct position.

She was leaving the study when she heard a car start up. She was at the top of the stairs when from the landing window she saw Stein's car roaring down the drive. She guessed he had gone to collect his father and that he would be away for hours. She knew then that it was the end, and that she would never see either of them again.

In her room she got out her suitcase and packed her belongings, trying not to think at all. But, her suitcase packed, ready to go, she just had to delay, to write Haldor a note. It meant lying to him, but caring for him as she did, that was better than any truth.

It was still early when Zarah left her note in Haldor's private sitting room for when he returned. She had thanked him for her stay, and told him of the pleasure it had given her to know him, then had gone on to explain that she had not intended to stay so long when she had first arrived, but that matters which she should have attended to in England had now become pressing. She had added a few words to the effect that she hoped to see him again before too long—but she knew that would never be.

She was far too numb as she left the house to have formed any plan. She had not gone very far, however, when the weight of her suitcase made her realise that she was going to have to find some sort of transport to take her to the nearest railway station.

Zarah set her case down on the pavement and rested her arms while she tried to remember if she had seen any sign of a taxi service, and to wonder what the odds were on any taxi driver wanting to be disturbed at this time in the morning. Then she heard the sound of a car coming from behind. The sound came nearer and the engine sound slowed, and foolishly, her heart leapt into her mouth.

But it was not Stein. 'Where are you going?' asked Rolv Fjeld in astonishment as he halted alongside her.

About to tell him 'Bergen' and beg a lift as far as the nearest railway station, Zarah saw him eyeing her suitcase. From experience she knew Rolv for a chatterbox. Should he be as free with his tongue with others, she had no wish to give any gossip food for speculating that she had either been thrown out, or conversely, that she could stand Haldor's house no longer and had done an early morning flit.

'I'm going to—Oslo,' she lied as she remembered that Rolv must be on his way to Oslo to do his sister's good works. 'I knew you'd be coming this way—I was hoping you'd give me a lift.'

'But of course,' said Rolv with a flash of his teeth, and jumped from his car to stow her luggage, which left Zarah with a few minutes to think up a few more lies.

'Uncle Haldor and Stein have gone fishing this weekend,' she told him when she was settled in the passenger seat and Rolv had started up the car.

'They left you to make your own way to Oslo!'

'Oh, they didn't want to,' she told him unblushing, 'but I insisted Uncle shouldn't break his plans for this weekend, and told him I was sure, since I knew you would be going to Oslo today, that you wouldn't mind giving me a lift. Uncle made me promise to telephone you last night,' she lied some more, 'only . . .'

'Ah,' Rolv took up, 'you tried, but I was out.'

'Yes,' she agreed.

'So—you're staying in Oslo? Or are you flying from there to England?'

Zarah barely hesitated. The pain in her heart over Stein rendered her fear of flying minuscule by comparison.

'I'm flying back to England,' she told Rolv.

Rolv offered to take her to the airport, but the journey impinged little on Zarah. She had thought she would stay numb for a long while, but pain racked her and nothing seemed to matter any more. What a fool she had been to think for a single moment that Stein might have some small caring for her. To accuse her the way he had proved just how much he did *not* care for her!

So much for thinking that he might have revised his low opinion of her. His opinion of her was where it had always been, at zero. To think, when they had lived in the same house all these weeks, that he could even *think* she might want to rob his father, let alone *say* it. It showed his opinion had not budged one iota—except to go down.

'What time is your plane?' Rolv, who had been chatting quite happily and appeared to need no more than the occasional 'Yes' and 'No' from her, suddenly asked a direct question and caught Zarah on the hop.

Taking a look at her surroundings, she saw a signpost to the airport, and realised that the airport could not be very far away. She glanced at her watch and went along with his belief that her flight was already booked.

'Er—in an hour and a half's time,' she lied.

'A great pity,' commented Rolv, a roguish twinkle in his eye. 'I was hoping I might give you lunch at my sister's home. But,' he sighed, 'they will want you to check in well in advance.'

Aware that his idea of 'lunch' and her idea of lunch were vastly different, Zarah sent him a smile for his sauce—for whatever else Rolv was, his having so willingly brought her this far endorsed his underlying kindness.

They parted at the air terminal where, bestowing a kiss to her cheek, 'Everyone does that at airports,' said Rolv with a grin.

Zarah felt she really liked him, as he walked away. He had gone from her thoughts, though, when, making enquiries about a flight, she was informed that because of freak weather conditions, all flights to England were cancelled for that day.

An hour later, the need to eke out her Norwegian currency no longer relevant, she had checked into a nearby airline hotel, with nothing to do but to wait until morning when, with luck, weather conditions in England would have improved.

With hours to fill, Zarah lay on top of her bed and tried to catch up on some missed sleep—only to find each time she closed her eyes that a picture of Stein, white-faced and furious, would appear, to make sleep impossible.

At eight, not enjoying the thought of joining the other diners, she rang room service. Common sense decreed she should fill her empty stomach with something, but she had little appetite when her meal was brought to her.

In the depths, she was trying to get some food down when, while endeavouring to think of something other than Stein, she unexpectedly found some peace in another direction. All at once she came to terms with herself over the issue that had so continually dogged her.

While she supposed there would always be a part of her that wanted to know, she suddenly knew that it mattered not which sister had given her birth. Margaret was the only mother she had known, and it had been Margaret who had guided her, tended her, and had loved her as though she was her own. For her part, she had loved Margaret as her mother, and nothing, not even if she had discovered she was Anne's child, could change that daughter's love she had for Margaret—that love which had grown in her over the years.

By ten o'clock any peace she might have found from the persistent questioning of whose daughter she was had long since been ruined. Thoughts of Stein were stubborn in her head, and just refused to be ejected. She killed time by having a bath, then went to bed. Somewhere around midnight she fell into an exhausted sleep.

Four hours later, her sleep was rudely interrupted by an announcement in several languages coming through the radio console in her room. Zarah came fully awake when the disembodied voice switched to English and advised all guests to make immediately for the nearest exit.

Realising that it was a fire alarm, she stayed only to don her housecoat, and left her room to bump into a confused-looking Japanese woman who was herding her family together.

'This way.' Zarah, feeling only a little less confused than the likewise-clad woman, took charge. She lost sight of them when, as they descended the stairs, they merged with other guests who had been roused from their beds.

The emergency was not *so* immediate, Zarah saw when she reached the ground floor foyer. For the foyer was crowded, no instruction given, it seemed, for anyone to assemble outside the hotel.

With people clustered about in twos and threes, she opted to stand in a spare space near a pillar. Many were dressed as she was, she observed, trying to get acclimatised to being robe-clad among the throng at just gone four in the morning. She had just noticed that one woman had brought her luggage with her when, suddenly, she froze. Then she could not see anything at all but the tall, broad-shouldered man who had taken time to don slacks and a sweater, and who stood out from all the rest.

Stunned, winded, for the briefest instant she thought that since she had Stein so much on her mind, her eyesight was playing her tricks.

No! It can't be! rioted through her brain. But it was. Even as her heart set up a tumultuous beating and her eyes widened, Zarah saw that, indeed, it was Stein. And what was more, he had just seen her.

She saw his head jerk back in utter astonishment. Then he was on the move. Purposefully he moved—towards her!

CHAPTER TEN

ALTHOUGH Zarah could not believe Stein was there when he should be miles away at home with his father, her instinct was to run. Somehow though, notwithstanding that her heart was racing like an express train, her legs felt too weak to take her anywhere. Then, as Stein came and stood squarely in front of her, it was too late to try to run.

She tried for some trite comment, but with her thinking powers in limbo, she was incapable of uttering a sound. Not so Stein. His astonishment had gone when for some seconds he just looked at her. Then, to reveal that Haldor must have shown him her note, he commented:

'According to my reckoning, you should be on your way to England—by boat.'

Considering that the last time she had seen him he had looked violent and ready to hit her, Zarah thought his tone remarkably casual. But she was more concerned with striving to appear unaffected to see him there, and latched on to his pointed 'by boat' to tell him, as coolly as she was able:

'One can't live in fear of flying for ever.'

She was saved having to add more when just then a couple of fire engines arrived. In the commotion of firemen entering the hotel, Stein took her arm and, imparting his view that the alarm was most likely no more than a technical fault in the hotel's fire alarm system, he guided her past one packed lounge to another less crowded one at the opposite end of the foyer.

By the time he had found them an unoccupied couch in

a relatively secluded spot, Zarah had taken a grip on herself. By then she had reasoned that to have left his father must mean that Stein had plans to fly out on business of some importance to his firm.

Abruptly such thinking ceased when he half turned and rested his eyes on her sleep-ruffled hair. Heartily then did she wish she had taken time out to use a comb. Then Stein smiled and, as her heart turned over, she had the hardest work not to smile back.

'So,' he said easily, 'what happened to make you want to forget your fear of flying?'

'Why should "anything" have happened?' she lightly tried to pretend that nothing had occurred to make her bogey of flying insignificant. But nerves grabbed her when Stein silently considered her with a steady stare, and she found herself going on, 'I—just decided I—wanted to go back to England, and—since I knew Rolv Fjeld was coming to Oslo . . .' she broke off at his sudden sharp look, and took another grip on herself, then continued, 'it seemed easier to come with him than to lug my case to the station and take a train to Bergen.' She had explained more than she meant to, but nerves again tripped her up, and saw her plunge straight on to ask something she had decided not to ask. 'So,' she said, 'what brings you to Oslo—where are you flying off to?'

Stein took his time in replying, and studied her for some moments before saying evenly, 'Had my plan worked, I would have been in Newcastle to meet your ferry,' and as Zarah's mouth fell open in shock, 'Your unreliable English weather,' he went on, 'has saved us both an unnecessary trip.'

Zarah's heart was by then beating so energetically she could hardly breathe. Stein had intended to meet her off the boat! He would have come after her! He had left his father on his own overnight to . . . Ice-cold reality hit her, and Zarah promptly fell off her spiral of hope.

'Your father . . .' she began quickly, cold common sense rapidly telling her that only if something had happened to his father would Stein come after her so urgently—though why he should, she did not stop to fathom, '. . . he's all right?'

'He's much better,' Stein reassured her. 'Thanks to you,' he went on, his look sincere, 'he is no longer in the suicidal frame of mind that overcame him when he lost Anne.'

'Thanks to me!' she echoed.

'You, Zarah, have given him something to live for.'

'*I* have?' she exclaimed.

Stein nodded, then paused, and without enlightening her, he decreed, 'We will leave the how and the why for a while—more particularly,' he paused again, and was never more serious, when he asked, 'will you please tell me what it was you were looking for when I found you at my father's safe yesterday?'

In a flash, Zarah was back to that happening nearly twenty-four hours ago. Pain assaulted her again to think that Stein had accused her the way he had. If she was in need of backbone just then, that memory, that pain, gave her all the backbone she needed.

'According to you,' she reminded him tartly, 'I found what I was looking for,' and straight away felt her stiffened backbone go to jelly, when he replied:

'I can't expect you to forgive me for what I said, or for what I so nearly did. I have no excuse,' he admitted, 'for the way I accused you, for the way I so nearly lost control and hit you. In my—disappointment—I reacted blindly,' he owned. 'There was no room in my head for logic.'

Weakened to know that he had reacted on feelings of disappointment, Zarah brought herself up short. Disappointed feelings or logic, the result was the same. 'What logic should there be?' she queried coldly. 'You caught me with my hand in the till . . .'

'That thought went with me as I drove to collect my father,' Stein further owned. 'And yet it just didn't tie up with the person I had begun to see in you.'

Her heart gave a lurch. Stein had started to doubt his accusation of her as he had driven along! It occurred to her that he was being amazingly open with her. Then she remembered that he had never held back when he had something on his mind.

'So you began to have second thoughts?'

He nodded, and sent her emotions all over the place, when he confessed, 'When I got my father home and he showed me your letter saying you were returning to England, I knew only that I had to come after you.'

Quickly Zarah lowered her eyes. 'To—apologise?' she asked, and found enough control to look up at him again. 'To apologise for what you thought?' she questioned a shade warily.

'To apologise,' he agreed, 'and to . . .' he broke off to clear a small construction in his throat, then started off afresh, 'I knew definitely after I read your letter that you were more the woman I had come to know than the woman I believed you to be when first we met.'

'With the opinion you held of me then at basement level, it—er—couldn't go any further down,' Zarah threw in with light sasrcasm, her comment, the way she said it, vastly at odds with the trauma that increased in her with every nice word he said.

'I deserve that,' Stein smiled, 'and more.' His smile disappeared as he said, 'When I checked your room and found your wardrobe bare, it only endorsed for me how wrong I had been. How could you be interested in the money that safe held when you knew that to leave

Norway in under six months would mean forfeiture of
your inheritance? How . . .'

He broke off as an announcement came over the
speaker. The announcement was repeated in English.
Zarah waited no longer than to hear that a technical fault
had been located and that it was safe for guests to return
to their rooms, to decide that she for one would feel far
safer in her room. Stein had once asked her to trust him,
but the plain fact was, she did not trust herself. She was
in love with him, and to be with him was bliss. But to be
with him was also weakening. He had come specially
after her, and would have come to England—to
apologise. What more could she want except what,
because he did not love her, she could not have?

The lounge emptied rapidly as the other guests
returned to their rooms. Zarah moved too, but only to
find, as Stein's hand stopped her, that he had other ideas.
She sank back to the couch intending to stay but a
moment.

'We have—a lot—to discuss,' said Stein, to squash any
idea she might have of offering some pleasantry and of
then bidding him good night and goodbye.

A glance round showed that they had the lounge to
themselves. Aware of the weakness he aroused in her,
even if he had removed his restraining hand from her
arm, Zarah once more strove to find some stiffening.

'What we have to discuss escapes me,' she remarked
coolly but saw from the quickly concealed glint in his
eyes that he did not care too much for her cool attitude.
That had never stopped her before, though, so if she was
to pretend she was the same woman she had been until
love for him had crushed her, it should not stop her now.
'But if it will prevent you from following me to England,'
she added, her voice growing cooler by the second, 'by all
means, let's have a discussion.'

For what seemed an age, Stein said nothing, but, as if trying to discover exactly what was going on inside Zarah's head, he just sat and looked at her. Then his gaze went to the stubborn set of her mouth, and when his grey eyes returned to pierce hers, he was rephrasing a question which he seemed determined to have an answer to.

'Okay, Zarah Thornton,' he said levelly. 'For a start, tell me what you wanted from that safe.'

She knew then that her only hope lay in trying to brazen it out. 'What makes you so sure I wasn't after some ready cash to pay for my flight home?' she asked carelessly. 'Ah,' she added as she remembered his thoroughness in checking her wardrobe, 'you've checked the money too—you know I haven't touched it. You know it's all there down to the last kron . . .'

'I have *not* checked it,' he cut her off, his level tone waning as aggression stirred. He had his aggression under control, however, as he told her quietly, 'I had no need to check the money.'

'Because—I forfeited those shares?' Zarah worked it out, and saw something akin to exasperation flicker across his face.

'Apart from that money,' he mastered his exasperation with her to detail, 'that safe contains only certain business contracts, plus a couple of legal documents. Which,' he went on, his tone softening, 'since you aren't interested in money, nor, since you were ready to give up those shares, are you interested in the business, it is natural for me to wonder—were you, Zarah, searching the safe for one legal document in particular?'

Her breath caught in her throat, he was so close. 'I . . .' she said chokily, desperately wanting her cool front back. 'D-does—it matter?' she tried to ask carelessly, wanting with all she had that Stein should return to the harsh uncompromising man whom she thought she could cope with better. This more gentle man—this man who now seemed ready to believe her, to want to understand, was rocking her foundations.

'It must matter—to you,' he answered. 'How otherwise would you—who I know to be honest,' he chipped another bit off her foundations, 'creep down the stairs in the early morning to go through that safe?'

'I've changed my mind,' said Zarah in a desperate effort to end the conversation. 'I don't want a discussion after all.'

She might have run from him then. But, anticipating her move, Stein had suddenly placed a hand over hers. That action alone told her that should she attempt to dart away, the pressure of that hand on hers would tighten. Speechlessly, she looked at him.

'Who are you afraid of hurting,' he asked, his tone more gentle than ever, 'yourself?'

Mutely, Zarah shook her head, and with his hand over hers, his touch warm, tingling, she had no hope to find stiffening again. She felt a mass of jumbled-up nerves, emotion, and love. Then she felt panic when Stein said quietly:

'You cannot hurt my father any more than he is hurt,' knowing all too well who it was she was afraid of hurting!

'I . . . He . . .' She had to look away. The realisation that he must believe in her sensitivity towards his father, her caring for Haldor, assaulted her emotions afresh. But, if that was not enough for her to try to cope with, Stein, waiting no longer for her to finish what she had started to say, suddenly took a long-drawn breath, and as though he was treading very carefully, he said:

'I'm trying with all I know not to hurt you, sweet Zarah. But,' he paused as her eyes flashed to his and away again, 'if all this, your attempt to learn all you could of Anne's friends when my father brought her to

Norway; if your silence on Saturday,' he went on as Zarah's nerves tensed as she saw where this conversation was heading, 'was because our visit to Gyda Wenstad proved fruitless, then . . .' he broke off briefly, to resume, '. . . then I can tell you that my father already knows—the truth of what you have been seeking.'

Zarah's tension suddenly snapped, and her shock was such that an exclamation escaped her of its own accord. 'He *knows*!' she cried, her eyes shooting to his.

'He has known from the very beginning,' Stein told her, warmth in his eyes when he added, 'I understand your lack of courage to ask him for the truth. Believe me, I understand that lack of courage only too well.'

'You—do?' she queried huskily.

'You were afraid of hurting him,' he stated. 'It is that same fear, in my case, fear of hurting you if—somehow— we are talking at cross-purposes, which makes me lack courage to tell you what my father told me yesterday.'

Had she been standing, Zarah was sure her knees would have buckled. Stein had never cared a jot what he said to her, or how much he hurt her! To hear him confess, when he had never been afraid to tell her anything, that he now lacked the courage to come straight out with what he knew, was staggering.

'Please, Zarah,' he said, when speechlessly she stared at him, 'please will you ask me what you want to know?'

Oh God, she thought, breaking out into a sweat. 'I . . .' she began on a gasped note, 'I wanted to . . .' she got a little further, but as her insides knotted up, again she halted, and was ready to chicken out totally. Then a moment of courage arrived. She grabbed at it. 'Whose daughter am I, Stein?' she asked.

Stein did not prolong the agony, but hesitated only briefly, then, *'Elskling,'* he said gently, 'you are Anne's daughter.'

Zarah closed her eyes, her hand turning in his to grip his hand tightly. Seconds elapsed when she was not aware of anything but that the question which had been a torment to her for so long had at last been cleared up. She came part way to awareness when she felt Stein's arm come about her shoulders.

'You are distressed? You did not want to know?'

The worried note in his voice, just as though any distress she suffered was his distress, brought Zarah to full awareness. She opened her eyes. 'I—d-don't know quite where I am yet,' she told him, and it was true. His arm about her, as if to comfort, was not conducive to her getting herself back together. 'It—was a sort of family joke between my mother—I mean, Margaret—and me,' she found she was telling him, 'that by mistake my birth certificate named Anne Margaret as my mother, and—not Margaret Anne, as it should have been.' She drew a shaky breath, and when Stein kept silent, inviting her to talk it all out, Zarah wanted to go on, her tongue seeming to have a life of its own. 'When my mother died and I had to attend to her personal belongings, I came across a marriage certificate that stated that the person who had married my father was Anne Margaret.' She swallowed, and began to feel a little less shaky. 'It just seemed too much of a coincidence that two mistakes had been made. On top of that, apart from the ages being wrong, the marriage certificate showed that the Anne Margaret who had married Felix Thornton was a sales assistant. Margaret Anne,' she told him, feeling a little more in charge of herself, 'worked for an accountant. She was even then plagued by arthritis and was incapable of standing all day.' Her voice started to tail off, and she ended, 'It just didn't add up.'

'You came to Norway to try and make it add up,' Stein prompted softly.

'I wasn't going to make a fuss,' she said quickly.

'You were going to ask Anne when no one was about—only you didn't know then that she too had died.'

'You believe I didn't know about her death!'

'Oh yes,' he replied with a gentle if rueful smile. 'I've had hours in which to do plenty of thinking. Hours in which to believe that Langaard might not have got around to writing to you of your inheritance before you left England. I've had ample time in which to be sure that he had *not* written to you. Time in which I soon knew that the letter my secretary had signed and sent to you in my absence had gone astray. I couldn't leave my father on his own in the state he was then,' he went on to explain. 'Which meant I had to dictate some quite considerable correspondence to my secretary over the phone. Clearly, with your English address strange to her,' he revealed what his deliberations had brought, 'she must have got some part of your address wrong.'

Weakened again, this time by Stein showing he had searched for answers concerning her which at one time he would not have paused to give thought to, Zarah stirred out of his arm, and let go his hand.

'I'm—all right now,' she said, and as Stein withdrew his arm from the back of her, 'I *was* looking for a legal document when you—er—caught me at your father's safe,' she thought she owed him a little explanation herself. 'I was looking for his marriage certificate.'

'You were looking for proof that he and Anne were married?'

She shook her head. 'I was looking for proof of Anne's name before she changed it to Kildedalen,' she corrected. 'It should have been Gentry, but if it was Thornton . . .' She had no need to go further.

'It would prove that Anne Thornton was your natural mother,' Stein ended for her, his tone compassionate as he added, 'Poor Zarah, if only you'd asked my father, you would . . .'

'How could I ask him?' she butted in, his compassion, his understanding of no help in her endeavours to get herself back to normal. 'It was all he could do to handle his grief. How, when it could be he didn't know Anne had a daughter, could I put the question in his mind, and add to his grief? Can you imagine what it would have done to him if in his subsequent questioning he learned that the wife he adored, and was so close to, had a secret which she had never felt close enough to him to reveal?'

'It would have crucified him,' Stein stated, and made her heart flutter when, in his conclusions, he said, 'You have a fine sensitivity, Zarah. Rather than cause him more pain, you instead held your tongue, and tried desperately to discover the truth by other means.'

She was more desperate just then to recapture some stiffening. If Stein made so much as one more kind remark, she had a feeling she might collapse completely. 'The way you were,' she grasped at what acid she could find to say a shade sharply, 'I couldn't very well ask you either.'

'If it's of any help,' he thoroughly demolished her by saying, 'you can't revile me any more than I revile myself for the way I treated you.' Swiftly Zarah found her lap of much interest. A moment's silence followed, then Stein went on, 'Had you asked me, though, I could not have answered any of what you wanted to know. I still believed you to be Anne's niece when my father gave me your note to read. When I told him I was going after you, and . . .' Abruptly he broke off. A few more moments passed, then he continued, 'It was then that he told me all there was to tell.'

Warmth coursed through her at the endorsement that he had intended to come after her *before* his father had told him anything. But she knew she dared not read more into it than that Stein had felt compelled to apologise in person for what he had thought when he had seen her holding that money, at the open safe.

'May I know,' she asked, 'what it was your father told you?'

'You have more right to know than anyone,' he answered firmly. 'In my view, you should have been told long ago.'

From there, Zarah listened intently as Stein related how his father, on a visit to England, had fallen in love with Anne. He had loved her fiercely, possessively, so that he could not bear the thought of returning to Norway without her. Anne must have been halfway to falling in love with Haldor, but while she wanted only the best for her hospitalised young daughter, she had been desperately hard up. When Haldor had invented a need of a temporary housekeeper, she had been pulled two ways until her spinster sister Margaret had assured her that she would visit Zarah in hospital every day.

Anne had gone to Norway and was soon heart and soul in love with Haldor. Having once been married to a man whose love had been so uncaring that he had walked out on her when she told him she was pregnant, Anne had delighted in Haldor's possessive love, and had been willing to do anything for him.

Haldor could not bear to be away from Anne for very long, and the idea of her returning to England made him terrified lest he might never see her again. She had, however, been about to go to England to see Zarah when Margaret had written that there was a chance of an operation which would enable Zarah to walk like other little girls. There were two snags, however. The surgeon lived and worked in France, and the operation and after-care would be astronomically costly.

Anne's gratitude, when Haldor insisted on going into colossal debt to pay for the operation, had known no bounds. Not to be a further burden on his finances, she had cancelled her planned trip to England.

'I didn't know!' gasped Zarah. 'I didn't know your father had paid for . . .'

'It pleased him to do it,' Stein assured her, 'but in the years that followed there were many occasions when the bank came near to foreclosing on the firm. Consequently, while he was striving to clear his debt, there was no money available for trips to England—or anywhere else.'

Zarah swallowed on emotion that through her, and for her, so much had taken place on this side of the North Sea that she had never known about. She had, as Stein had once said, lived in luxury, while they had had to scrape along.

'There's been so much sacrifice made for me,' she said huskily, feeling suddenly humble. But only to see anger in Stein, which had been remarkable by its absence, when he retorted shortly:

'Dammit, woman, Anne was your mother! I'd have thought far less of her, and my father, had they done nothing.'

'I'm sorry,' she apologised quickly, not sure what she was apologising for, except that she much preferred Stein when he was not angry. 'Go on,' she urged, 'I'm sorry I interrupted.'

'So you should be,' he said, but there was no anger in his voice, more of a smile, she thought. He was serious, though, as he went on, 'Margaret gave up her career, and in those following years she somehow took on the role of your mother. Perhaps Anne intended to claim you one day, but it seems that she slipped into agreeing to leave things as they were for the time being. However it was, by that time, any money my father could spare was sent to England for your upkeep. Make no mistake, Zarah,' he continued, not giving her time to dwell on his last statement, 'Anne loved you.'

'She must have done,' Zarah agreed slowly, and felt a glow inside that it must be true, or why else would Anne have let the husband she loved so much too come near to financially ruining himself?

'She loved you,' he repeated staunchly, 'but she knew Margaret loved you also. So that by the time we moved from a small flat into a property with room for a family, Anne, in her happiness with my father, knew it would break Margaret's heart to let you go. In all conscience, she just could not take you away from the beloved sister who had cherished you as if you were her own.'

More gladness filled Zarah's heart that it seemed Anne had never forgotten her, but had wanted her with her. 'There wasn't—room in your new home for both my m . . . Margaret and me?' she asked tentatively.

'There was,' he confirmed, 'and Anne suggested that you both come over. But Margaret wrote back to reveal—what she had been silent about—that her arthritis was much worse, and that she would never be able to survive the rigours of a Norwegian winter.'

'Poor love,' said Zarah softly, 'English winters were bad enough for her.' She fell silent, but surfaced from the sad memory of her mother's pain, and had to ask, 'Why, when Anne began to be a bit better off, did she never come to England to see me?'

'Love, for you *and* Margaret, kept her away,' Stein answered. 'For years she had to be content with photographs from Margaret and twice-a-year letters from you. She was afraid that to see you might have her—despite her love for her sister—unable to leave and not take you with her.'

Zarah digested what Stein had just told her, and

realised that along with everything else he had filled in
for her, there could be little she did not know. 'So, instead
of coming to England,' she finalised, 'Anne—and your
father—made certain, by sending that quarterly
allowance, that I wanted for nothing. That same
quarterly allowance,' she inserted a shade uncomfortably
as another memory struck, 'which you objected to having
to continue when you took over the running of the firm.'

'That quarterly amount doesn't seem so large now,'
Stein shrugged it aside.

'It would have made business life much easier for you
had you not had to keep on paying it, though,' Zarah
pressed.

'I could have done with the money myself,' he had to
admit. 'I needed all I could lay my hands on to get the
company up off the ground.'

'But your father refused to allow you to stop the
payments?' she guessed.

'It incensed me,' he owned, sending her a smile that
did funny things to her insides, 'when I explained how I
was going to have to gamble everything in a financial
scheme which would either ruin us or give us a chance of
prosperity, and still he wouldn't give his permission to
cancel that banker's draft.'

'You—er—never asked why?'

'My father had let slip that, although paid to Margaret
because of your age, the money was mainly for you. I
stopped asking why, when he reminded me that it was
the least we could do for Anne's niece, since it had been
Anne, out of the goodness of her heart, who'd suggested
that the remains of my boyhood be spent in a secure
home with them, rather than the existence I was living
with my mother and various—"uncles".'

'But that didn't stop it—rankling?' she said, her heart

going out to him for the rough time he must have had until Anne had stepped in.

'It infuriated me,' Stein confessed, with not a sign of fury or a return to the way he had been the last time this subject had come up for discussion. 'Especially was I infuriated,' he admitted, 'when Anne delighted to tell me that her niece had now left school and was in perfect health. There was I still working all hours to drag the firm up off the floor, while this young Englishwoman, in perfect health, just refused to get off my financial back and earn her own living. Only now I know of the delicate surgery you had in infancy have I realised why Anne was so proud of your perfect health.'

'I—couldn't go out to work,' defended Zarah, going on quickly. 'Aside from being brought up believing our income came from a trust fund my grandfather set up, it just wasn't possible for me to leave my—Margaret—for more than a few hours at a time.'

'I never knew how ill she was,' Stein said soothingly. And, to make Zarah's heart crash against her ribs, he told her warmly, 'Had I known anything of what I now know, your welcome to my country would have been vastly different.'

Oh, if only it had been different! If only . . . Abruptly, Zarah switched her mind from that which could never be and drew hard on her last reserves of strength.

'Well, it's all out in the open now,' she told him brightly. 'If you haven't done so already, you can cancel that quarterly payment. The first thing I'll do when I get to England will be to get myself a job, and . . .' Stein, his look incredulous, his voice sharp, cut her off.

'You still intend to go back to England!'

'Why, of course,' she said, slightly bewildered.

'But you can't!' he said forcefully. 'I won't let you,' he told her categorically.

'You won't let me!' echoed Zarah, but even as her eyes widened, and she tried to deny the thrill that possessive statement brought, she was pushing herself on to his arrogant level to tell him, 'Good heavens, Stein, surely you haven't forgotten that if I leave in under six months those shares revert to the family!'

'Devil take the shares!' he snarled, to her astonishment. She was still trying to recover, her memory clear that he had been so keen to have her shares that he would have given her a written undertaking to pay for them, when he almost sank her without trace, by claiming shortly, 'You *are* family!' Zarah was making mammoth efforts to get herself together, when he went on, 'Why in God's name do you think Anne left her will the way she did? Why do you think she wanted you to stay in Norway for six months?'

'A-apart from wondering if—to have left me so much—meant she might be closer to me than an aunt,' she confessed haltingly, 'I hadn't thought about the six-month stipulation very much.'

'Then think about it now,' Stein said grittily. 'No,' he amended, 'I'll do it for you—I've had hours in which to see how it was.'

Up to her neck in confusion, 'I'd be—glad if you would,' mumbled Zarah.

She was all attention when Stein told her his findings. 'With Margaret dead, Anne was disturbed that you were alone. She knew her own time was short, but, while she wanted you here, she did not want you to witness what would have been a painful end for her. Added to her worry about you was the constant fear that my father might not want to live after she had gone. It's my belief,' he continued sternly, 'that Anne's last act was to try to ensure that you would come to Norway where, in six months, my father might grow to love you as a daughter, and would therefore watch over you like the father you never had.'

'Oh, Stein,' Zarah said chokily, able to see that it could well be as he had said. 'But,' she went on, her heart full, 'it's taking your father all he has to keep himself going, without . . .'

'Not any more,' Stein disagreed. 'While at one time it was for my sake that he did not end it all, it is you who have given him a reason to go on living. Don't you see,' he went on when she did not look convinced, 'that while in those first few days of you coming to us he was full of remorse because—in his posessive love for Anne, he felt he had deprived her of you—he . . .'

'He couldn't help that!' Zarah protested. 'He paid for my operation, and did all he could to . . .'

'He didn't see it that way,' Stein interrupted. 'All he could think of in his remorse was that while Anne had not hesitated to take his son into their home, his heart had not been big enough to enable him to find a way of having Anne's daughter in that home too.'

'But everything was against it!'

'It was,' Stein confirmed. 'But it wasn't until you'd been with us a few days that he began to see that Anne, by wanting you to stay in Norway for six months, had given him her trust. Had given him a chance to earn her forgiveness—and yours.'

'There's nothing to forgive,' Zarah said promptly. 'Please tell him that. I was happy with Marg . . .'

'Tell him!' exclaimed Stein, and was sharp again when, no two ways about it, he told her, 'You can tell him yourself. When we get back to . . .'

'The only place I'm going back to is England,' Zarah cut in, sharp herself; that—or surrender. Only to have Stein bark:

'Even though you know we don't want you to go!'

'You yourself said your father is better now than he was,' she retorted, fully conscious that although Stein had said 'we don't want you to go', it was for his father's sake that he did not want her to leave. 'I know it's going to take time,' she added, when Stein studied her aggressively, 'but he'll go from strength to . . .' Again she was sliced off. This time, though, she was left gasping, when Stein snapped bluntly:

'I'm not asking you to stay for his sake, but for mine!'

For the past half hour, Zarah had used everything she could find to mask her inner feelings. But to hear Stein say that it was for *his* sake that he wanted her to stay, left her without the smallest hope of covering the emotions which those words had let loose. Even while, regardless of what he said, it *had* to be for his father's sake that he wanted her to stay, her mouth fell open. And even while she was aware of Stein's gaze fully on her, she had no chance at all to hide, or halt, the rush of emotional scarlet that flamed her face.

She averted her eyes when she saw the way his brows shot up and how shaken he looked to realise from her crimson colour that his statement that he personally wanted her to stay had created something of a storm in her. Terrified, because if his statement itself was not an indication that he had gleaned some notion that she cared for him—and would, for his sake, stay—Zarah knew she had to pull out all the stops. At all costs, she had to prevent Stein's clever mind, fuelled by witnessing the flush of colour to her face, from taking him up a path which it must not go!

At pains to disabuse him, as her colour receded, she flicked him a careless glance. 'Why should I do anything for your sake?' she drawled loftily.

'I've given you every reason to want to do exactly the opposite,' he answered thoughtfully. But before she could tell him 'Good, that's just what I intend to do' he was going on mildly—too mildly, for him, 'You came to Norway with one aim in mind: that aim, to discover whose daughter you were. Tell me, Zarah,' he enquired with slow deliberation, 'why were you ready to leave without finding out what we both know was so important to you?'

Panic lunged at her again, and she was too strung up then to have a ready answer. By some miracle, though, she remembered how it had all come together in her hotel room. 'It just didn't seem so important after all,' she was able to tell him then. 'Suddenly I knew that, since Margaret had been the best mother in the world to me, it just wasn't so important who my natural mother was.'

Stein looked away from her, but she was sure it was not disappointment in her answer which made him silent for long moments. Before she could find much relief from panic, though, his eyes had returned to her, and, his tone still mild, he asked:

'Your reasons for leaving in such a hurry, then, had nothing to do with my last accusation being more than you could take?'

'Really, Stein,' she managed to evade, 'I'm used to your accusations!'

'So why leave in such a hurry?' he stumped her by asking, and pressed on when she had no answer. 'You did leave in a hurry, didn't you, Zarah? Indeed, so anxious were you to get away, your anxiety even overrode your fear of flying.'

'I've already told you,' Zarah made gallant efforts to stay calm, 'Rolv Fjeld was coming to Oslo. It seemed far more convenient to hitch a lift with him than to take the train.' Her second wind arrived, she grabbed at it, and had even found a touch of sarcasm when she tacked on, 'Although, deep in my heart, I must have known there was some good reason why I should avoid airports—and airport hotels.'

'Now why,' he tossed back, not a whit stung by her acid tone, 'should you wish to avoid me?'

'When I've more time,' she snapped, 'I'll write you a list.'

Stein smiled. 'We're not going anywhere,' he gave her an open invitation.

'For a start,' Zarah took him up on his offer, 'you're overbearing, arrogant, accusatory, and . . . and . . .'she ran out of steam, and was very nearly flattened when he took up:

'And possessive,' he added to her list, his smile gone, 'in my love.'

For one sublime, totally insane moment, she thought Stein meant that he was in love with her. Common sense, cruel and heartless common sense, knocked that ridiculous idea squarely on the head. Pride was her only ally then, when, with an ache in her heart, she forced herself to ask:

'You're in love—with someone?'

'I'm consumed by love,' Stein added to the pain in her heart. 'So much does this love I have consume me,' he turned the knife, 'that there are times when I just can't think straight.'

'My condolences,' Zarah said brittlely in the hope of shutting him up. She just could not bear to hear more. But he showed no sign of shutting up, and caused her more pain, when he went on to confide:

'I never wanted it to be like that. I'd seen enough of my father's possessive love of Anne to know that no woman was going to have me listening for her footsteps, or watching the clock when she was a minute later coming home than I thought she should be. I just knew I wasn't going to love like that.'

More because some comment seemed called for, plus pride decreeing she should show him how entirely unaffected she was, Zarah offered an offhand, 'But—you do?'

'I do,' he confirmed positively—and promptly sent her into a spin when he straight away followed up, 'Before I knew it, there was I clock-watching. When each afternoon she went out for a walk, I wanted her back home. When she went out to dine—with another man—I just could not rest until she returned.'

Oh God, she thought, and started to tremble inside. She knew she should listen to the common sense of her head, but her heart seemed to have a will of its own. It insisted on contradicting any previous notion that she wanted him to shut up. Contradictory too, she knew she just had to bear to hear more.

Her mouth felt dry, but she just had to ask, 'She—she was staying—in your home?'

'My father's home,' Stein corrected her, and at the look of high tension on her face, he leant forward and took a gentle hold of one of her shaking hands. 'I didn't know to begin with that I was on the brink of the greatest love of my life—the only love of my life,' he told her softly.

'You—didn't?' Her voice was a breath of a whisper, and she almost melted at the wonderful warm look his eyes held when, as if taking encouragement from the husky thread of her voice, and from the fact that she had not attempted to snatch back her hand, Stein answered:

'All I knew at the start was that I was being assaulted by emotions I didn't comprehend. I kissed my love in absolute fury—and found I liked her response.'

'You did?'

He nodded, his eyes gentle on hers as he said, 'That kiss weakened me, and sent me on the way to changing my pre-formed opinion of a beautiful Englishwoman.'

Zarah's heart gave a desperate lurch. 'She's—English—th-this . . .'

'This woman I love,' Stein took over, 'is English, and beautiful. Can you wonder at my rage when, about to revise my opinion, she proves she is all I had previously thought, when I find her rifling through my father's desk?'

'She was looking for . . .'

'I know, and understand all that now,' he said softly. 'At the time, though, I was such a mass of differing emotions, I didn't understand myself. There was I, enraged one minute, taken aback the next to see the shine of tears in your eyes when Anne's photograph reminded you of your mother—I determined never to be taken in again. Yet, again before I knew it, jealousy, something I had never experienced, was there to undermine me.'

'You were jealous!' Zarah exclaimed.

'Possessively so. I neither liked the feeling that came over me when, in my presence, you arranged to dine with some other man, nor the fact that after that dinner you told him you'd look forward to his second phone call.'

'Rolv?'

'The same,' grunted Stein, his smile gone. 'I didn't know where the hell I was when you blithely announced that you were going away with him.'

'It wasn't like you thought—that overnight stop, I mean.'

'So I soon found out. Dear God, when I think of you innocently driving off with Fjeld, when I think of what might have happened to you . . .'

'I—it . . .' Zarah butted in, wanting Stein to smile again. But she had no defence, and with wonder in her heart at all she was hearing, she had not the tiniest wish to argue with him. 'I'm sure nothing would have happened—had I had to return to his sister's home,' she said, and went on quickly, 'but as things turned out, your father sent you after me, and . . .' Something in Stein's expression made her break off.

'It seems,' he murmured, 'I have to own to a small dishonesty.'

'You!' she exclaimed.

'Me,' he confirmed. Zarah was ready to forgive him anything when his smile came out. 'My father didn't send me,' he confessed, to her astonishment, and he admitted, openly, 'When you weren't at breakfast that Sunday, such a restlessness overtook me that I knew I had to do something constructive or go insane. I came after you.' Zarah was still trying to take that in when he told her, 'I wouldn't have let you return to Fjeld. I'd have come back for you when I'd cooled down. But you asked me for a lift and we went home together. A week followed where I fought hard against this possessive feeling I did not want,' he went on. 'But I knew by Friday that the odds were against me. When that night my father announced that he was going fishing, and you were so lovely in your impulsive attempt to ease my mind about him, that barrier I was trying to erect promptly crumbled.'

'You—of-offered to take me to see Fru Wenstad,' Zarah put in unsteadily.

'I'd given in,' he reiterated. 'I wanted you to myself. To drive you to Gyda Wenstad's seemed an ideal way to have you alone, and by my side for some hours.'

Her heart full to overflowing, her thoughts flew back to that visit to Fru Wenstad. It seemed to Zarah then, with Stein being so open, that she had no cause to hide anything. More, she wanted to tell him everything.

'I think I've been more than a little muddleheaded lately,' she confessed. 'But the only reason I wanted to see Olav Langaard was to find out if Anne had confided

anything about me to him. Only she hadn't, and I thought
I was never going to know. Then Rolv told me that Fru
Wenstad had known Anne before she married your
father, and all I could think of was that perhaps Fru
Wenstad knew what name Anne had used before she
married him.'

'But she didn't, and that,' said Stein, in full understanding, 'was the reason for your silence all the way
back to Dalvik.'

'I'm sorry,' Zarah apologised softly. 'You asked me to
trust you, to tell you what was wrong,' she rushed on,
wanting it all said quickly, 'and I knew only that I must
not tell you, but that if you didn't let up—I might do just
that.' She took a gulped breath and raced on, 'And then
you kissed me and—and a little later, well—I suppose I
got a bit shy . . .' Her voice faded altogether at the tender
look Stein gave her. 'Anyway,' her voice picked up
speed, 'then you repeated "Trust me" and all I could
think—and I confess you hadn't left me with very much
brain power—was that you were only m-making love to
me so I would tell you my secret.'

'Come here,' he said throatily. The next moment she
was cradled in his arms. 'I sorely wanted to know what
was troubling you,' he said softly against her ear, 'but
only because I felt shut out and wanted to help, and have
a need in me to share everything with you. There was no
thought in my head for anything once I had taken you in
my arms, though. All I knew then,' he explained, 'was
that I ached to have you respond to my kiss as you once
had before.'

'Oh, Stein!' sighed Zarah, and with her head tucked
into his shoulder, her face hidden from him, she just
could not hold back the question that burned on her
tongue. 'Does that mean—you l-love me?' she asked.

An exclamation in Norwegian hit her ears. Then Stein

was turning her until he could see down into her face.
Then, his expression never more sincere, he declared,
'You have me in such a state, Zarah Thornton, that if I
have not told you in so many words of the depth of my
feeling for you, then I will believe you. But if you have
still not understood how it is with me, I will say plainly
that I love and adore you with everything that is in me.'

'Oh—Stein!' Zarah cried tremulously.

'I am right, then,' he asked, and seemed suddenly
tense, 'you do feel a little something for me?'

'I f-feel—more than a little something for you,' she
replied shyly.

'A little—love?' he asked, still tense.

'You have not understood *me*, I think,' she answered,
the smile on her mouth telling him he had no cause for
alarm. 'I'm just not the type of woman who would listen
to all you have said, without trying to stop you, if I did not
feel a—very great deal—for you.'

Still he did not appear satisfied. 'Will you tell *me
plainly*, woman,' he growled, 'what it is you feel for me!'

'I love you,' Zarah said. Stein waited to hear no more,
but, held in his rib-cracking embrace, she had no wind
left to tell him more.

Minutes passed while Stein seemed contented just to
hold her like that, but would pull back to look into her
face and see love reflected in her eyes, then hold her
tightly against him again. Then he kissed her, and kissed
her once more, and in between kisses he was telling her of
his love.

Zarah touched the side of his face with her hand, and
kissed where she had hit him, and apologised for the
blow, and then Stein told her how, in his love, he had
been utterly devastated to have evidence that she was a
thief when he had seen her by the open safe holding that
confounded money.

'I wasn't thinking straight,' he freely confessed. 'Fear, when I love you so completely, that I might yet strike you, and so nearly did, made me leave that study, and quickly,'

'You then decided I was not a thief,' her eyes stayed on him to smile.

'I knew it the moment some semblance of sanity returned,' he smiled back. 'Though you did steal my heart,' he told her tenderly.

'You can't have it back,' she laughed.

Unable to resist it, Stein kissed her, and for a while there was no room in Zarah's head for anything. Then Stein was breathing more words of love in her ears, and telling her of his initial frustration when his father insisted on delaying him from chasing after her—to tell him why it was that she had every right to inherit Anne's shares.

'He believes I have a right to them!'

'As I do,' Stein said emphatically. 'Your natural mother willed them to you. But,' he smiled adoringly, then set her heart pounding, as he said tenderly, 'you will be my wife, *min kjaereste*, and everything I have is yours.'

Her eyes felt moist, and she just had to savour those most beautiful of words. 'Your wife,' she said dreamily.

'You will marry me?' he asked, and even though she was sure there could be no doubt about her answer, she saw a thread of anxiety in him as he waited for her to reply.

'Yes,' she said simply, and had her lips claimed. It was a gentle kiss, but a fire kindled in her as his kiss deepened, and Stein's ardour increased. Suddenly, though, he checked, and he was putting her gently away from him.

'My love,' he said, his voice thick in his throat, 'there's a quite desperate need in me to kiss you, and to kiss you, and to go on kissing you.' He took a much needed strengthening breath. 'But,' he went on, 'once I do let go of the very small control you have left me with, I'm not certain when we shall surface.'

Stein had made a nonsense of her senses, without his words throwing her into more delighted confusion. But, with her pulses hammering away, she made valiant efforts for clear thinking.

'Your father?' she queried.

'Exactly,' he said, giving her a love-filled look. 'He has more faith than I that I shall act like a gentleman. But, since neither of us is taking a plane, shall we check out now and return to Dalvik where my father is waiting for us?'

'He's waiting for *us*!' exclaimed Zarah, and catching on, 'You told him you would bring me back?'

'I told him I would have to go where you went,' he owned, 'and that I was going to marry you?'

'You did?' she asked faintly.

'Why else do you think he delayed me to tell me all he did?' Stein smiled, his smile becoming a grin as he went on, 'My father can be crafty in his own way. He confessed he had felt something was in the air, and that he'd made at least one attempt to push us together.'

'Good heavens!' she gasped, startled. She was even more amazed when Stein revealed:

'I can only suppose he must have caught something in the way I looked at you when you weren't looking. But he was definitely on to me when—knowing full well my being in Oslo that first time was none of his doing—you told him that not only was I there with you, but that we'd been on an organised sightseeing tour together—something which he knows I can't abide.'

'You hate organised sightseeing tours?' she gasped, and had to laugh when, comically, he nodded. When she recovered, she reminded him, 'You said your father had made at least one attempt to push us together. When was that?'

'He'd no intention of going on a fishing weekend with Brage Juvkam,' Stein told her, 'but when instead of learning to know each other, he felt that we seemed to be more avoiding each other than anything else, he decided that to leave us alone in the same house might bring some results.'

'The crafty . . .'

'What did I tell you?' laughed Stein. He had drawn her to her feet, adding, 'He has the same true affection for you, *elskling*, that you have for him.'

Stein kept an arm about her shoulders, as he took her through the foyer *en route* to collect their luggage from their rooms. They were waiting for the lift when Zarah asked, 'He won't mind, then—your father—about you and me . . .?'

'Mind!' he exclaimed, and turned her in his arm to observe the trace of uncertainty in her brown eyes. 'Oh, my dear, dear love,' he breathed adoringly. 'He'll be overjoyed when he knows you've agreed to be my wife. Do you know what he said when I told him I was going to marry you?' Her eyes fixed on Stein's warm and loving grey eyes, dumbly Zarah shook her head. 'He said, "For your sake, I hope she accepts you, but for my part, it would give me much happiness to have a legal right to call Zarah my daughter'.'

'Oh, Stein!' Zarah whispered.

The lift arrived and the doors opened. Stein bent his head and bestowed the gentlest of kisses on her mouth. 'Come, my heart,' he said huskily. With his arm fast about her, they stepped into the lift, and ascended.

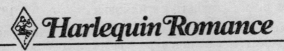
Harlequin Romance

Coming Next Month

2863   BRIDE ON APPROVAL   Elizabeth Ashton
Sancia desperately wants to be free from her restrictive upbringing,
yet she can't bring herself to escape by way of an arranged
marriage—not even to the charming Italian count chosen for her!

2864   THE GOOD-TIME GUY   Rosemary Badger
Her boss's relentless pursuit causes problems for office manager
Sarah Ames. She's come to Brisbane with her sights fixed on a
career and has no time for a man only interested in playing games!

2865   IMPULSIVE ATTRACTION   Diana Hamilton
During their first magical meeting in the moonlit woods, it doesn't
seem to matter that he's a mysterious itinerant sculptor, while
she's a respectable bank manager. But by daylight, the differences
between them threaten to destroy their love.

2866   SLEEPING TIGER   Joanna Mansell
There's nothing sensible about social butterfly Lady Sophia's
suddenly inspired decision to follow a teacher to the Sahara so she
can do some worthwhile work with him there. It certainly changes
her life—but not quite in the way she expects....

2867   EXCLUSIVE CONTRACT   Dixie McKeone
Against all the professional counseling rules about not getting
romantically involved with a client, Janet Talbot enthusiastically
sets out to rescue an unusually charming housebreaker from a
life of crime!

2868   AN OLD AFFAIR   Alexandra Scott
Only her father's urgent need for money sends Arabella seeking
help from the man she had loved and mysteriously lost seven years
ago. His price for giving it is high—one Arabella isn't sure she
wants to pay.

Available in October wherever paperback books are sold, or
through Harlequin Reader Service.

In the U.S.
901 Fuhrmann Blvd.
P.O. Box 1397
Buffalo, N.Y. 14240-1397

In Canada
P.O. Box 603
Fort Erie, Ontario
L2A 5X3

**For the millions who can't read
Give the Gift of Literacy**

One out of five adults in North America
cannot read or write well enough
to fill out a job application
or understand the directions on a bottle of medicine.

**You can change all this by joining the fight
against illiteracy.**

For more information write to:
Contact, Box 81826, Lincoln, Neb. 68501
In the United States, call toll free: 1-800-228-8813

**The only degree you need
is a degree of caring**

LIT-A-1R

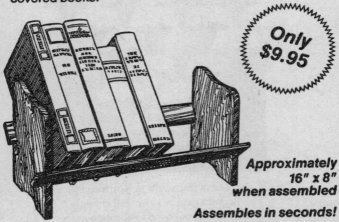

It was a misunderstanding that could cost a young woman her
virtue, and a notorious rake his heart.

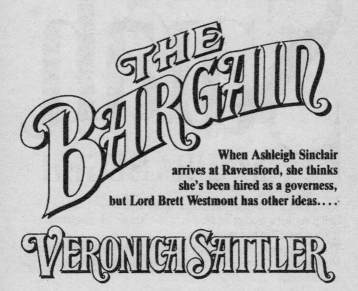

THE BARGAIN

When Ashleigh Sinclair
arrives at Ravensford, she thinks
she's been hired as a governess,
but Lord Brett Westmont has other ideas....

VERONICA SATTLER

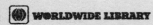

Sarah

MAURA SEGER

Sarah wanted desperately to escape the clutches of her cruel father.
Philip needed a mother for his son, a mistress for his plantation.
It was a marriage of convenience.
Then it happened. The love they had tried to deny suddenly became a
blissful reality... only to be challenged by life's hardships and brutal
misfortunes.
